D0500223

The Heart Behind
The Hero

We hope you enjoyed the stories shared in "The Heart Behind the Hero".

Be well!

karengola

[signature]

The Heart Behind The Hero

A Heartwarming & Inspirational Collection of True Firefighter & Paramedic Stories from Across America

by

C u r t   &   K a r e n   Y o d e r

Stoney Creek Press
Trabuco Canyon, California

www.firestories.com

We would like to thank the following publishers and individuals for their permission to share and print their stories. (Note: Material from the public domain, and material written by Curt Yoder and Karen Yoder, are not included in this listing):

Jokes R Us. Excerpted from *Sirens for the Cross* by Tommy Neiman & Sue Reynolds. © 1998 Tommy Neiman and Sue Reynolds. Published by Embrace Communications. Reprinted by permission.

Wall of Fire. Excerpted from *Angels of Emergency* by Donna Theisen and Dary Matera. © 1996 Donna Theisen & Dary Matera. Published by HarperCollins Publishers. Reprinted by permission.

(Permissions continued on page 197)

Publisher's Cataloging-in-Publication
(Provided by Quality Books, Inc.)

The heart behind the hero : a heartwarming &
    inspirational collection of true firefighter &
    paramedic stories from across America / [compiled
    and edited by] Curt & Karen Yoder. -- 1st ed.
        p. cm.
        LCCN: 00-90616
        ISBN: 0-9700487-2-6

        1. Fire fighters--United States--Anecdotes.
2. Fire fighters--United States--Biography.
3. Allied health personnel--United States--Anecdotes.
4. Allied health personnel--United States--
Biography. 5. Emergency medical personnel--United
States--Anecdotes. 6. Emergency medical personnel
--United States--Biography. I. Yoder, Curt.
II. Yoder, Karen.

TH9118.A1H43 2000   363.3'7'0922
                QB100-483

© 2000 Curt & Karen Yoder

All rights reserved. No part of this publication may be reproduced, stored in a retrieval system or transmitted in any form or by any means, electronic, mechanical, photocopying, recording or other-wise, without express permission of the publisher.

Publisher: Stoney Creek Press
        P.O. Box 70
        Trabuco Canyon, CA 92678-0070

Cover Design & Photo by: Michael Salas www.msalas.com

Printed in the United States of America

With loving dedication to my dad
John Allison Yoder
Battalion Chief
Los Angeles County Fire Department
1954-1983
Fallen in the Line of Duty

Dear Dad,

When I think back on the many ways you have influenced me, I have trouble knowing where to begin.

As a young child, I remember sitting in the hose room getting a haircut from one of the firemen—feeling so proud to have you for my dad. I remember coming home from work in my high school and college years, regularly finding a couple of my friends hanging out with you in our garage—talking with you about being a firefighter.

Your generous and warm attitude influenced many of my friends, as well as your sons, to choose this great profession.

Growing up, I was always so proud that you were my dad—and my pride continues to grow as I recall these special memories of you. I only hope that I have become the type of man that would make you proud.

Your son,

Curt

Contents

I.   The Heart Behind the Hero

Calls that Touched the Lives and Hearts of Firefighters and Paramedics across America

II.   Those Who Forever Touch Our Hearts

Memorable Moments that Forever
Tie Our Hearts to Those We Serve

III.   On a Lighter Note

Stories We Like to Tell Over and Over Again ...

IV.   Rookies

The Heart of the Fire Service ...
There's a 'Rookie' in all of us ...

V.   A Tribute to Our Fallen

*A Special Tribute to Those
That Lost Their Lives in the Line of Duty*

Roll of Honor 157

*Our Fallen Brothers & Sisters
1981-1999
As recognized by the
National Fallen Firefighters Foundation
National Fallen Firefighters Memorial
Emmitsburg, Maryland*

Acknowledgements

We are extremely grateful for the continuous encouragement and support we received from our family, friends, contributors and production team in writing *The Heart Behind the Hero*. Without the help of these wonderful people, and God's gentle guidance, this book would not have been possible.

We wish to thank the following:

Our parents, *Ed & Celeste Keyser and John & Bonnie Yoder*. Their loving examples of commitment to marriage and family are our model for the kind of marriage and family life we strive to maintain. We truly appreciate the sacrifices they made for each other, and for us, and thank God everyday that we were blessed with such loving parents.

Our children, *Andrea, Cami, Casey and Michael* for the love and joy they bring to our lives.

Chris Yoder, our brother, who beat all odds to turn his life around and has been an enormous help and blessing to our family. We are so proud of you, bro!

To all of our family members who dedicated their lives to serving others in this great profession. My father, *John Allison Yoder*, whose inspiration led many to this great profession. My Uncle Dale, *George Dale Yoder*, who retired after serving with the Los Angeles County Fire Department (1956-1972) and the State Fire Marshal's Office (1975-1992). My older brother, *Craig Yoder*, who is currently serving as a Battalion Chief with the Los Angeles City Fire Department. And my younger brother, *Chris Yoder*, who assisted the Los Angeles County Fire Department as a fire control laborer.

To all of our very special friends and neighbors, whose daily love, inspiration, and dependability we truly rely on—you know who you are ...

Laurie Sullivan, Janet Salas, Debby Wright, Rhonda Larson and Ken Keyser, for their keen eyes and thoughtful critiques in assisting with editing stories.

Michael Salas, for designing our cover and inspiring us with his infectious enthusiasm and artistic savvy. Michael, you are a true professional who is a sure-bet to make a mark in the film industry.

Larry Jackson of Heidelberg Graphics, for his diligence and dependability in setting the final text and meeting our tight deadline.

Mary Ellis of the National Fallen Firefighters Foundation, for her encouragement and support of *The Heart Behind the Hero.* Thank you, Mary, for allowing us the opportunity to include the names from The National Fallen Firefighters Memorial in our book.

To all those who sent stories to *The Heart Behind the Hero.* Although we couldn't possibly use all the stories we received, your faith in our project and kind words are very much appreciated. We thank you from the bottom of our hearts.

To all those in the Costa Mesa Fire Department who supported *The Heart Behind the Hero* from its inception, especially:

Thom Caldwell, for giving so much of his time to everyone in the Costa Mesa Fire Department with his computer knowledge and expertise. Thank you, Thom, for helping us with our web site and all of our computer related challenges.

Rich Merritt and Doug Prochnow for their business input and creative insight.

Tom Stewart for spending countless hours in front of the camera ... move left ... move right. Yes, that really is Tom on the cover.

We know we have not listed everyone who has touched our lives and been a support to make this book possible, but truly appreciate everyone who offered their guidance and words of encouragement. May God bless you all.

Curt & Karen Yoder

Foreword

There are givers and there are takers in this world and firefighters are truly givers. They give of themselves, on the job and off, and sometimes they give their lives to protect the lives and properties of others.

Every firefighter is an individual, each with his or her own background, lifestyle, religious belief and personality. But, when it comes to our profession, we are all very much the same.

When firefighters are called to duty, we do so without hesitation because it is the job of firefighters to be the first responders to every disaster and emergency, whether natural or manmade.

Firefighters know they can count on each other whether they are the best of friends or they have never met. This is the bond that every firefighter shares. It is a bond that knows no geographic boundaries. And it is this strong kinship that guarantees, without question, that firefighters can count on one another no matter what must be done to get the job done.

Firefighters rarely talk about the dangers that are an ever-present part of their job. We don't talk about the suffering we see and the pain we feel in the course of our normal workday. If you are not one of us, you don't know this. But this is who we are. This is what we do.

We are not immune to the physical dangers that often accompany our duties—and we are not immune to the heartbreak and emotional trauma we face when helping our fellow human beings in their time of need.

In an era when heroes are hard to find, few would dispute that firefighters are America's heroes. At a time when bravery is in short supply, firefighters demonstrate the essence of bravery. Although some suggest that the notion of duty has been forgotten, firefighters epitomize what duty really means—and in a society where sacrifice is seldom practiced, firefighters are too often called upon to make the ultimate sacrifice, putting the lives of others ahead of their own.

The Heart Behind the Hero brings to life the daily emotions and feelings of America's firefighters and paramedics—the pain of their losses, their camaraderie and their dedication.

My sincerest thoughts and condolences go out to the thousands of families and friends who have lost a firefighter in the line-of-duty. Nothing can erase the grief and sorrow you feel over your loss, but I hope and pray you can take comfort in knowing there was abundant meaning in their lives.

Take heart in knowing that they were engaged in an endeavor that is a measure of human greatness and that they will always be remembered for their courage, honor, and selfless dedication.

Let us never forget that the humanity and compassion embodied by these brave men and women lives on.

Alfred K. Whitehead, President
International Association of Fire Fighters (I.A.F.F.)

Introduction

*I provide a faceless, nameless service to a
community that rarely knows how much they
need me. If I am called from a sound sleep to
sacrifice my life attempting to save the life or
property of someone I do not know, I will do so
without regret.*

Jon McDuffie, Firefighter

Firefighters and paramedics have long been admired
for their courage, compassion and humanitarian-
ism. They move heaven and earth to prevent disaster
or save a life. As did heroic Paramedic Jana Knox,
when she risked her life to scavenge through ruins and
human remains to find survivors after a bomb ripped
apart the Alfred E. Murrah Federal Building in Oklahoma City.

Abundant thanks to Mr. Webster for defining *hero*
(noun) *as a person noted for feats of courage or nobility,
especially those who risk or sacrifice his or her own life.*
I am privileged to befriend so many of these heroes. As
the wife of a fireman and as a civilian who depends on

emergency services to remain a telephone call away, I say they are, indeed, heroes. But ask most any firefighter or paramedic if they feel heroic and they will likely disagree. The men and women who continually witness unmasked tragedies and come to the aid of many, simply consider it part of their job.

And although much self-satisfaction comes with the ability to help people, firefighters and paramedics also must live with the devastation and sorrow from split-moment decisions and tragic circumstances that are all too often beyond their control. Without hesitation, Firefighter Doug Faulisi crawled into a burning smoke-filled home, successfully rescuing a small child, only to discover later there were *two* children in the same bedroom—one he had missed.

Admiration, courage, compassion and respect— these are some of the words used to describe individuals who endanger their own lives to save others. Blessedly, they are human—and are vulnerable to the pain and suffering of those they serve. In chapters, *The Heart Behind the Hero* and *Those Who Forever Touch Our Hearts*, firefighters share the pain and emotions they experience while holding a dead child in their arms or consoling the wife of a dying man. These are the heartbreaks they must endure, and often times never forget.

Heartbreaking and physically exhausting experiences are only a portion of the unique work dynamics. In each twenty-four-plus hour shift, firefighters share meals, cook for each other and sleep side by side. This provides an opportunity to reveal the true nature nature of oneself, albeit heroic or humble. In chapters *On A Lighter Note* and *Rookies*, firefighters share their bond of brotherhood with stories that have been cultivated by these close living arrangements.

. *A Tribute to Our Fallen*, the final chapter, is a collection of heartfelt messages written in memory of firefighters that paid the ultimate sacrifice. The *Roll of Honor* lists all those who lost their life in the line of duty, as recognized by the National Fallen Firefighters Foundation.

Each story shared in *The Heart Behind the Hero* offers a glimpse into the lives of the real people behind the rescue dramas. Some stories will make you laugh, while others may make you cry, but all will warm your heart as gentle reminders of our human frailty and the true courage of these men and women who risk their lives each day.

This book is dedicated to all firefighters, paramedics and their families for their compassion, dedication and sacrifice. And to the memory of all whom lost their lives in the line of duty.

Karen Yoder

The Heart Behind the Hero

Calls that Touched the Lives and Hearts of
Firefighters and Paramedics across America

Is It Worth It?

The hopeful man sees success where others see failure, sunshine where others see shadows and storm.

O.S. Marden

We fight every day to change what many consider inevitable. Often we lose. In the field we remain composed and stoic. Professionalism dictates we remain aloof. We feel anything but.

We've all had those days, those calls. We go home and ignore those we love for fear of venting the frustration. We are drawn to the darkest corner to mull the defeats. It's a crucial time. In those silent moments we wage a war within and we ask: Is it worth it?

Then, we look at the scales others pan and remember yes, I made a difference ...

... to a two-year-old little girl, and the parents who nearly lost her.

The patio door was ajar, the pool gate not quite latched. On scene first, the rescue truck stuck in traffic, I rush through the gate to see a crying mother stooped over a sodden form, a mop of curls and clothing plastered wetly to a tiny, fragile body. Demeanor alone moves mom aside as I lift her gently and listen, feel.

Nothing.

I force back my own tears and blow a breath through her blue lips as my left hand prepares to compress. An eternity, thirty seconds in real time, passes with breaths and compressions. The wail of approaching sirens is nowhere near as gratifying as the wracking cough I elicit from the lass in my arms.

Her eyes flutter open; her cry is the sweetest sound I've ever known.

... in the existence of a life-long friend. His wife was driving home when she suddenly crossed lanes and careened into a guard rail. Myself and a first re-sponder, who was driving two cars behind her, call it in on the radio and rush to her aid.

She's unconscious and breathing. My friend immo-bilizes C-spine and I begin my primary.

Without warning, she crashes, no breathing or pulse, and we pull her from the car as gently as possible to begin CPR. The rescue arrives and the driver has the defib at our side in a matter of moments. The third shock delivers us a heartbeat and shallow breathing. Load and go.

I get a card from her every year, on the anniversary of her almost-death.

... for one very frightened, very sweet elderly woman. Her neighbor heard a weakened cry for help and called 911. I park the rig in front and we gain access through the kitchen window. Her voice is very frail and muffled, but we follow it to the bedroom closet where she had fallen hours earlier.

She's alert and conscious as we lift her on to the cot and strap her in while our third man gets vitals. We suspect stroke. Maneuvering the cot, I watch as her fear, confusion and weakness overcome her. She apologizes continuously through the tears, shaking so bad we have a hard time putting the oxygen mask on. I opt to ride with her, with the new EMT in the jump seat to monitor. The new guy handles the radio report to the Emergency Room, as I scoot off the bench and kneel next to her.

I bend to whisper words only for her. Was that so-and-so in that picture on your wall? Is she your granddaughter?

As we wheel her out of the rig at the end of the nine-minute ride she's a different woman, laughing and telling us about her grandchild and an old high school friend.

There will always be more bad than good. It's the nature of what we do. To those who've never experienced the elation of these particular successes, the scales seem to favor the losses. But we who understand—we who do—know this couldn't be further from the truth. When we save one life, we affect so many more ... the family and friends who would have been left behind. When we stop to count the wins and losses, and count the family and friends of those we save, we realize our efforts *do* balance the scales in our favor, as we do not, ever, affect only one life—we touch all.

Michael R. Chase, Firefighter/EMT
Nantucket Fire Department
Nantucket, Massachusetts

A Life Saved

A single event can awaken within us a stranger totally unknown to us. To live is to be slowly born.

Antoine de Saint-Exupery

A round four-thirty in the morning my engine company, Engine 3, pulled up to the burning two-family home on James Street. Fire ran rapid through all three floors. Dense black smoke poured out of every window in the front, and halfway to the rear. The fire had started in the front of the house and moved toward the rear at such a quick pace, we couldn't imagine anyone still being alive in this inferno.

People yelled, "There are two children trapped inside!" My officer ordered the deck gun to the front of the building and ran around to the rear of the house to attempt a rescue. From left to right, I immediately began spraying the front of the building with our deck gun. I used up the five-hundred gallons in our tank within a minute. The fire was so intense that my effort had little effect. I immediately jumped down from the fire truck and ran around back to see if I could help my Captain in our rescue attempt.

When I got to the back door, Captain Moore was nowhere to be found. Another firefighter informed me that he went inside to make an attempt at rescue. The door he entered was filled with the blackest smoke I had ever seen. I began to crawl into the building through the smoke-filled passage to find and assist the Captain, only to bump into him a few feet inside. The Captain and Lieutenant Muscanelli from Rescue 1 were dragging out an adult male. I helped them get the man safely away from the building. The two officers promptly started resuscitation efforts.

At that point, I heard a woman behind me screaming, "My baby! My baby!"

Her desperate calls made my blood run cold, and the hair stand on the back of my neck. I turned to her and asked, "Where's the baby?"

"In the bedroom!" she cried.

"Don't do it," Captain Moore yelled, as he stood and grabbed me by the shoulder. "It's going to blow any second!"

I looked at the building and could see he was right. But something inside me said, "You can do it."

I masked up again, wondering if I could pull it off. I knew the woman's voice would haunt me forever if I didn't at least try.

As I went toward the rear door, black smoke was being pushed by a wall of fire that began to spread across the kitchen ceiling. I knew that I could make it to the bedrooms, but I wouldn't be able to return the same way. I'd have to go out the bedroom window. Hopefully, with a child in my arms.

Four minutes had passed since we pulled up in front of this nightmare. I had to make a life-or-death decision, alone.

The clock ticked. No more time to think. I was on my feet, running through the kitchen toward the front of the flat—without a hoseline. The heat knocked me down to my knees and I began crawling. As I entered the bedroom, I stood up and immediately began to look and feel for my window exit. The visibility was only a few inches due to the dense smoke, so I ran my gloved hands along the wall hoping to find the window. My right hand found the edge of the window frame. Then I bumped into a large piece of furniture. As I felt along and around this stereo cabinet or bookshelf, I realized it was blocking the window, my only way out!

My chest began to burn with fear. Visibility had become more a state of mind than fact, and I suddenly realized I would have to retrace my steps back through the kitchen, which by this time had to be completely engulfed in flames.

For the first time, ever, I feared for my life.

Pushing the fear to one side, I began to search the room. Back on my knees, I crawled and felt the area around me. I located the side of a bed and quickly found the top.

Nothing.

Without hesitation I crawled around to the opposite side of the bed. Suddenly, as I crawled, my hand rested upon a small leg. It startled me and for a moment I couldn't move. Still blinded by the smoke, I gently ran my hands up the torso to the head and thought, *a small child.* My emotions raced between being horrified and elated. I had to get this child out of there.

Cradling the child in one arm, I crawled toward the bedroom door, only to discover the kitchen had begun to light up. The fire enveloped the entire ceiling and had moved down the walls. I had no choice but to continue crawling, through the fire-engulfed kitchen, toward the rear exit. The heat was intense, but I continued on, finally reaching the rear porch.

We did mouth-to-mouth resuscitation and CPR on the child until the air ambulance arrived and airlifted him to a Bronx hospital. There the child received further treatment and survived.

Later I learned there had been another child in the same room. One I had missed. Through the days that followed, I hovered between elation and depression for the life saved, and the life lost.

Since that day, I realize that life is fleeting, and can't be taken for granted. If I had known about the second child, and had taken the extra time to search, I wouldn't have been able to save either of them, and probably would not have survived myself. Both people I helped that morning are alive and well today.

I truly believe that this rescue was a stepping stone to make me more aware of my own mortality and that of others. I developed a deeper appreciation for the little things in life. Days that used to be *nice spring days* turned into, *Beautiful Spring Days!* I tend to be a bit more cautious and more aware of my surroundings. I have no desire to stare death in the face the way I did that morning.

Not long after the rescue, a reporter doing an article on the department asked me how it felt to be

a hero. My response: "I don't know about being a *hero*,
but I *do* know it feels great to be a fireman!"

Doug Faulisi, Firefighter
Schenectady Fire Department
Schenectady, New York

Weight of the Badge

It is certainly wrong to despair; and if despair
is wrong hope is right.

Sir John Lubbock

"KCF907 dispatching Rescue 2 to a report of
motor vehicle versus bicycle, corner of Cato
Lane and Barlett Road. 907 needs one EMT to call the
station and personnel to respond," the radio in my
truck barked.

Usually not serious, I thought, as I turned the
Wagoneer and flipped on lights only, Code 2 response.

A second transmission came through. A first
responder on the scene, frantic, said only four words,
"Step it up, now!"

I switched on the siren and floored the gas. When I
arrived on scene a minute later, a sweeping glance told
the tragic tale of a life ended far too early. Three

Emergency Medical Technicians knelt in a growing pool of blood, performing CPR, knowing the futility of their efforts.

A mostly finished case of beer, some of its cans fallen to the ground beneath the open driver's door, lay by the side of the road. Two officers held back one of the victim's friends from the intoxicated driver, screaming his hatred of the man he did not know until minutes ago.

I quickly moved in to relieve the medic on compressions, so he could ready an airway and O2. My palms pressed into the yielding flesh of the victim's sternum and I knew that there was no life left to this young, once strong, boy. Even through the large amounts of blood, which I guessed was roughly half his body's volume, I could see he was much younger than me ... early, maybe mid-twenties. Every compression forced a few more precious drops to the ground. Someone took over for me and I stripped off my gloves preparing to run escort for Rescue 2. Dropping my gloves to the ground, I hoped to leave behind the memories of what I had just seen. Even with all precautions, the blood of the innocent victim was now part of me.

Not for the first time, not for the last.

The rushing, the grabbing of equipment and cot, making radio calls to the hospital to prepare them for the emergency victim. I knew it was all a show. The faces of my comrades said that they knew too. This boy was no longer alive.

There was nothing we could do, but we could *not* do *nothing.*

I raced ahead of the ambulance to block the one major intersection, then fell in behind to make sure they had enough personnel to unload. As I pulled in to the parking bay behind them, I saw they were set.

Sitting there in the parking lot, in my Jeep, I looked from the blood on my wrists and hands, up to the badge on my chest. My fingers touched the well-worn metal crest and I wondered if what I had just seen was worth the weight this badge sometimes carries? What a temptation to be rid of the weight.

A shadowy figure emerging from a police cruiser caught my attention. The young man started toward the door of the Emergency Room, then saw me and turned toward my truck. In the faint lights of the bay, I saw he was one of the victim's friends. He stopped ten feet away, and looked up. Tears rolled down his cheeks.

In the silence, his whisper washed over me like the rumble of thunder.

"I knew you couldn't ... I mean ... hey, thank you for trying," he said gently, the sound of his voice breaking.

He turned and walked toward the ER to hear what he already knew.

I looked back down to the metal symbol on my chest. It now stood for something more than uncompromising responsibility. It represented dedication, and the opportunity to make a difference in the hearts and lives of others. With renewed conviction, I knew that, indeed, I could bear the weight this badge carried.

I started my truck and headed home. Back to my family who'd have to understand my silence one more time.

Michael R. Chase, Firefighter/EMT
Nantucket Fire Department
Nantucket, Massachusetts

Emotional Heroes

Great occasions do not make heroes or cowards;
they simply unveil them to the eyes of men.
Silently and imperceptibly, as we wake or sleep,
we grow strong or weak; and at last some crisis
shows what we have become.

Brooke Foss Westcott

Justin, my fourteen-year-old son, worked as an administrative aide in the attendance office at Columbine High School when the shooting began at 11:15 a.m. on April 20, 1999. He was compiling attendance sheets when he looked up and noticed kids running past the office window. Looking at the clock, Justin realized class shouldn't be out for another thirty minutes. He went over and opened the window.

Amidst the frantic screaming of his fellow students, Justin yelled, "What's going on?"

"They're shooting at us in the cafeteria," a voice shouted from the fleeing classmates.

Shooting? In the cafeteria? thought Justin. *This must be a senior prank.*

He ran down the hall to check it out. As he approached the cafeteria, he heard the gunshots and was startled by the shatter of a window just ten feet away.

This, whatever this was, was for real.

Justin, now sensing the same terror as the others, ran back to the office and, knowing it was my day off duty from the Littleton Fire Department, frantically called me at home.

"Dad, there's someone shooting at us at school. I'm leaving, now," he told me, his voice shaking, "Please come and get me at Michael's house. I've got to go. Please hurry!"

I had never heard that desperate tone in my son's voice before. My body shook from anxiety and my mind spun with unanswered questions. What was he talking about? Shooting? The frightened tone in his voice bolted through me as I recalled incidents from other parts of the country where kids had posed as snipers with other children as their targets. Was this happening here?

As I turned the corner into my nephew Michael's neighborhood, I saw scattered groups of teenage kids walking around, some were crying, but all had looks of sheer terror and confusion. The crying held each other, while the others walked in groups with looks of bewilderment and shock on their faces. Just then I realized the magnitude of the events taking place, and how lucky Justin and his cousin were to be alive. When I reached Justin, I asked if he had seen or knew the whereabouts of Ben, his older brother, also a student at Columbine. Justin didn't know.

As the tragic event unfolded I knew I had to get Justin home. My wife had heard the news and was on her way home before I had even picked up Justin. My nephew stayed with his parents and I took Justin home, where my wife waited. I embraced my tearful wife, both of us still in deep shock and frightened for our oldest son. I knew I needed to get back to the school to find him, and help in any way I could.

When I arrived at the high school I met with Operations Chief Ray Rahne. An undetermined number of students and teachers were still inside the school and unaccounted for. We were told that some kids were being murdered, execution style, by two students from Columbine. Ben was still missing, as were children from other firefighter personnel and rescue workers.

Even in the face of chaos and personal tragedy, we knew we had to do our job. The survival of the students and teachers were at stake. If we were to make a difference in the outcome of this tragic event, a plan had to be swiftly and carefully devised. Although my thoughts never left the heart-wrenching concern I had for Ben, who was still missing, I knew that I had to focus on the task at hand. It was critical to the success of our rescue efforts. I was assigned to a task force of engines from multiple jurisdictions in a unit based four blocks from the school. Although too distant to maintain the contact I would have desired to stay close to Ben, Columbine remained in plain sight and we were in constant radio contact with the command center at the school.

Maintaining our focus and not allowing our personal distractions to influence us, our task force began preparing for a possible fire breakout due to explosive devices being located throughout the school—a staggering number that later totaled to more than ninety devices. We developed an additional operational division as part of the existing command structure, and organized a fire suppression plan in case of an explosion. Luckily, there were no explosions, and we did not need to implement our plan.

Needing to maintain a connection to my family during this time, I used the engine's cellular phone to make repeated calls home. I hoped Ben would turn up there. Around three o'clock in the afternoon, I found out my older son had made it home and was okay. I was relieved from duty to go check on him.

My two boys were safe at home, away from the horrors still taking place. It sent a wave of overwhelming relief through me, yet my heart still ached for my sons who remained in a suspended state of disbelief and shock, struggling with the reality of what was taking place. Emotions, at this time, swirled and no words or consolation could erase or lighten the load of grief impacting our family and community. For the time being, I knew my sons would be okay and we would all sit and talk as soon as someone would stop stirring up this anthill of emotion and tragedy.

My family now was safe, but the crisis continued at the school. My wife, realizing the profound internal instinct all firefighters have to assist during times of emergency, encouraged me to return to Columbine.

Many of the initial response crews were exhausted, both emotionally and physically, when I returned to the school later that afternoon at about five o'clock. Plans were already in place to release these crews to Critical Incident Stress Debriefing teams. The department started calling back off-duty people to relieve the initial crews, allowing those that were involved during the traumatic chaos to participate in the Critical Incident Stress Debriefing.

I went back on scene to aid Battalion Chief Jeff Christ with the reassignments and left the scene at nine that night. I was taxed as well, and yet had no exposure to the horror and traumatic upheaval that the initial crews had witnessed first hand. I admire and hurt for those people ... I'm so proud of them all!

On this horrific day, I witnessed the unity of the people in our community at a time of great distress. In the face of adversity, I saw genuine heroes.

I saw medics compassionately holding teenage kids in their arms.

I saw the administration of medical care completed with the utmost professionalism, despite the dulling effect tears can have on hand-eye coordination.

I saw the walking, emotionally wounded children comforted by uniformed officers as if these kids were their own. Perhaps, in a way, they were.

Three of our fire paramedics who first responded to the scene, specifically Monte Fleming, Jerry Losasso and John Aylward, risked their lives as they pulled two victims from within the school as gunfire exploded around them.

I witnessed one of our off-duty paramedics, Captain Brian Simpson, who also has a daughter at Columbine High School, sacrifice the search for his daughter to render critical care to a gunshot victim that presented herself to him.

While doing our jobs to ensure the safety and care of hundreds of victims, we overheard comments such as "We have to get some of these kids out of here," and, "Someone go hold that crying girl," and, "Would someone find out if OUR kids have been found and are indeed okay?" I heard countless offers to help in any way, shape or form from so many people, on and off duty, from countless jurisdictions. Rescue efforts during the Columbine tragedy were an amazing tribute to the kind of people that make up the compassionate family of Fire, Police, and Emergency Medical Services.

Our rookie firefighters made me especially proud that day. I saw so many *kids* grow up. I saw a number of young firefighters step up to the plate and give aid in any capacity they could. Whether they were starting intravenous lines, dressing a wound, directing an ambulance to the quickest route to the hospital, or merely standing by in a task force assignment awaiting orders from the Operations Officer. I saw rookies, who had been on the team six or nine months, presenting themselves to the public they serve with the compassion and professionalism of any fifteen- or twenty-year veteran.

There are many scars left from this horrible day, from so many beautiful people lost. The school has broken and scarred windows covered with plywood. Holes in the ground remain where cable companies set up their utilities to cover the whole fiasco. There is a park in town, two blocks from Columbine High School. The grass is trampled to the bare dirt by many people who, in their own process of healing, came to present flowers, stuffed toys, prayers and poems in memorial to *the teacher and students* who lost their lives. They paid tribute, not only to the ones that died, but also to those that must live with the sights and sounds of what they experienced. The park's groundskeeper said, "I don't know how long it will take for the grass to be green again."

The many tears shed at the memorial will help the grass grow tall, strong and green again. The school will be painted and repaired. The windows will be reglazed.

As for the healing of human spirits? Provided we, too, can grow from the tears shed. Provided that we, too, can remember the kids that died, and comfort those that survived. Provided we can, in all aspects of our service community, live up to the expectations of not only our community, but our own peers. If we can continue to go beyond the boundaries of theological acceptance and love, focus on communication with our children, and be accepting of expressive ideals and perceived adversarial diversity ...

We, too, can heal.

Barry "Skip" Wilson, Captain
Littleton Fire Department
Littleton, Colorado

The Thirteenth Jump

*Humility is not renunciation of pride but
the substitution of one pride for another.*

Eric Hoffer

S mokejumping has been in existence since the
experimental use of parachutists to enter otherwise
unapproachable terrain proved successful. The U.S.
Forest Service Smokejumper Project became fully
operational in the summer of 1940.

My rookie year as a smokejumper began in 1960,
at the base in Cave Junction, Oregon. At Cave Junction
the wildland fire suppression training is some of the
most intense and grueling of its kind in the nation. For
four weeks we participated in parachute drills, emergency landings and countless practice 'let downs' for
the times when we would need to land in trees instead

of on the ground. By the completion of training, I was ready for anything.

The fire season started with the usual small fires in different areas throughout the Umpqua National Forest. The Umpqua includes nearly a million acres within the western slopes of the Oregon Cascades. Extraordinary geological events in the Umpqua National Forest produced its beautiful distinctive landscapes and breathtaking scenery. Douglas Firs, as tall as some jump stories, blanket the mountains and river canyons.

On this hot August morning, we were dispatched to a *two-manner*, which is smokejumper talk for a two jumper fire. I was ready to make my thirteenth jump. As lucky a number as any, I guess, and like all jumps it offered the promise of an exceptional experience. Even with the exaggerated confidence of a young man, there is no doubt that it takes strong will, determination and downright guts to parachute into a burning forest.

Ideally, the goal would be to drop into a clearing, but in a tree laden Oregon forest this goal isn't usually achieved. More often than not we end up having to grapple down a hundred-foot tree before the real work begins. Our job is to trudge through the smoke-filled forest to combat man's natural enemy ... fire ... and then hike out to safety.

My partner Owen and I made our jumps upwind from the fire, and I got hung up at the top of a tall Fir, dangling from its branches rather than the intended descent to *Mother Earth.* I snagged out my hundred-and-ten-foot rope, tied off to my chute, and dropped the rope toward the ground—which I couldn't see due to the thick canopy of limbs blocking my view.

Owen, my jump buddy, was on the ground about the time I started to come out of my harness to make my descent.

"Tex, don't come down. Your rope ends fifty feet off the ground," Owen yelled up.

Douglas Firs don't have many limbs the first hundred feet or so, which would have left me dangling in open space with a big step down. I retrieved my rope, climbed down about sixty feet through the limbs, tied off to a limb, and then made my let down. No big deal. We put the fire out, retrieved our chutes and packed out.

The Forest Service, like a lot of big organizations, likes to have full-scale, detailed reports. Jim, the project air officer, an older jumper in his mid-thirties, conducted the After Action Report and asked me about the tree landing.

I was more than proud to explain the 'easy' landing, shrugging off the difficulties as mere inconve-
niences. Being in my early twenties, I thought even if
the sun didn't rise over our heads each morning we
could get the job done. After all, we were probably the
roughest, toughest specimens of mankind on the face
of the earth. I accepted that with pride and bravado. I
gave Jim my report, proudly mentioning that it was my
thirteenth jump and felt I was due a little excitement.

"I remember my thirteenth jump," he said.

"Yeah?" I asked, anticipating a story of thrill and
excitement. I imagined a fierce tumble out of the sky, a
raging fire below—him against nature at its toughest.
"What was it like?" I asked excitedly, sensing a kinship
and camaraderie that only us smokejumpers could
understand.

"I was twenty-one years old," he said with hardly a
show of emotion, "It was July 1944. Holland."

World War II—a month after D-Day. You could hear
my bubble burst, and the wind leave my sails, when
he told me.

A young man, jumping behind enemy lines, far
away from home. This soldier was not only concerned
with the danger of landing in trees or rocks, but also
had a hostile enemy shooting at him with the intent to

kill. I could imagine bullets whizzing by, knowing the odds of surviving and returning home were very slim.

As I faced this veteran, this man of true courage, this man who truly deserved respect—humility and honor secured a place in my life.

Gary Welch, Smokejumper
Cave Junction
Class of 1960

Wall of Fire

Courage is fear holding on a minute longer.
George S. Patton

There was a massive forest fire up in the rim country that burned for nearly a month. It consumed twenty-eight thousand acres of Tonto National Forest, including the home of famous Western author Zane Grey. Firefighters and medics from all over the state banded together to battle what became known as the *Dude Fire.*

I arrived home from my honeymoon and was immediately sent into the fray. My first assignment was a wild one. A crew of prisoners recruited to battle the blaze were overcome by what we call a *blowup.* That's when the fire shifts direction and overtakes the firefighters. The prisoners had been trying to clear the underbrush from bulldozed fire lines, sections of land cleared in order to stop the inferno's spread.

Five prisoners and a female corrections officer were killed. Others were injured. I was ordered to respond to the highly dangerous area and try to rescue whoever remained standing.

"There could be more blowups," my captain cautioned. "Be careful."

I drove along a forest trail as far as I could until I reached a cabin near a partially burned-out area. I left the vehicle and began searching for the victims on foot. Suddenly I heard an overpowering noise that sounded like a half-dozen freight trains barreling toward me. I turned and froze in shock. It was a blowup! A wall of fire fifty feet high was coming directly at me! It was consuming so much oxygen that a gust of wind nearly sucked me into the flames.

Medics and firefighters are given a heat-resistant aluminum foil-like tent that we're supposed to use in such situations. The theory is, you hit the ground, cover yourself with this fireproof material, and allow the zillion-degree fire to burn over the top of you. The questionable technique makes no concession for the fact that as the fire passes, there's no air to breathe. On top of everything else—intense heat, crashing trees, paralyzing fear—you're supposed to hold your breath.

Despite my misgivings, there was nothing I could do. I was trapped. I spread out the tent and hit the ground, fully aware that this was exactly what the perished prisoners had tried to do. I figured I was history. My new wife was going to be a widow one day after our honeymoon. Just as I was about to crawl under the foil, I heard someone yell. I looked back and saw six paramedic-firefighters emerge from behind the cabin. They were carrying a man on a backboard and appeared to be totally exhausted.

"Come over here!" they yelled. "We need your help!"

I jumped up and ran toward them, ignoring the mountain of fire that was about to overtake me. It didn't matter. I was there to save lives. I was going to do my job or die trying.

As I ran against the wind, I immediately started gulping for air. It felt like I'd run a mile instead of a few feet. I realized then why the six medics were having so much trouble with a single patient. There was so little oxygen left in the air that any exertion left them gasping. They'd already carried the victim for two hundred yards and had little energy left.

I made it to them and immediately lifted the board with my fresh strength. Glancing back, I saw the wall of fire make a sharp left, as if it were turning a corner. It was like God had blown it away with His breath. Alternately taking turns and collapsing from exhaustion, we lugged the injured prisoner up a hill where a helicopter was supposed to land. The ground was so hot beneath our feet, we couldn't even pause to rest. With barely any oxygen to breath and the smoldering earth scorching our boots beneath us, it was a long, draining climb. Taking courage from each other, we powered onward and somehow made it to the top just as the chopper arrived. The prisoner was flown to the hospital and survived.

We, however, remained on the hill very much in danger. When we climbed down the opposite side, I was shocked to see nearly two-hundred paramedics and firefighters huddled together in a small bulldozed clearing. The theory is that the fire, finding no fuel in a cleared area, will leave it alone.

We danced the hotfoot in that clearing and watched the fire rage all around us. It shifted directions a half-dozen times or more, sometimes whipping toward us, while at other times mercifully retreating in the opposite direction. Its helter-skelter pattern was caused by the fact that the massive fire was creating its own wind currents, which blew around us in every direction.

Normally a forest fire burns the underbrush so fast that it ignores the larger trees. This one was so hot that the trees started exploding like bombs. They'd smoke for a while, and then with a thunderous whoosh would burst into flames like giant matches.

We also began to hear a series of piercing whistles followed by ear-shattering booms.

"Propane tanks," a fireman beside me explained.

The tanks were mounted outside the numerous cabins in the fire's path. As they heated, they'd vent their pressure and then explode.

After three agonizing hours, the fire consumed the forest around us and headed off like a hungry monster to seek more food. When the ground cooled enough to let us escape, we discovered that the paint on our fire trucks had blistered, and the plastic parts, including the headlights, sirens, and flashers on the roof, had melted.

I was awarded a Medal of Valor for my activities that day. The six other paramedic-firefighters were given similar awards from their departments, including being selected as Firefighters of the Year. Despite honors, the psychological aftereffects ran deep. I'd been an avid camper all my life. In fact, I'd just spent my honeymoon camping in the forests of Utah and Nevada. After staring down that wall of fire, though, I wasn't able to set foot in the woods for more than a year.

Howard Clark, Paramedic
Arizona
As told in <u>Angels of Emergency</u>
By Donna Theisen and Dary Matera

Flashback

Do not look back in anger, or forward in fear,
but around in awareness.

James Thurber

Editor's Note:

Firefighters and rescue workers are often faced with
unexpected, traumatic circumstances. The participation
and observation of these events, such as fatal car
accidents, bombings, shootings, or the death of a fellow
firefighter, are outside the normal range of usual human
experiences, and can inhibit a person's normal ability to
cope with stress. Although the severity of emotional
reactions to such events can vary from person to person,
it is very common for people to experience some degree
of difficulty following a traumatic event.

Since the development and universal implementa-
tion of Critical Incident Stress Debriefing (CISD), most

firefighters have the immediate resources to help them cope with the emotional trauma related to difficult calls.

CISD teams comprise professional Psychological Debriefers who meet with those directly involved or witness to a critical events—usually immediately following the incident. The following story shares how one firefighter's traumatic experience influenced his life for many years ... before CISD training and participation in psychological counseling positively changed his life. The children's names have been changed.

The flashback was rather sudden, especially since I hadn't had one in more than a year, and no nightmares that I could recall in the last two.

We were on the way to the hospital with our patient, a little boy who was hit by a car, when I began to feel a little shaky. Tears welled up in my eyes.

Suddenly ...

... I see a little red car surrounded by people. Everything is going slowly, and I hear sounds that I guess are voices. Moving is like going through molasses, and people are shouting, "Get in the back! Get in the back!" as they point to the car's rear door. I pull it open, and there's the kid. Just a little one, lying in a pool of blood around his head. His eyes and mouth are open. Blood is dribbling from his right nostril.

I feel like I've been hit in the chest with a sledge-hammer; the air gets knocked right out of my lungs. I reach forward, and feel resistance—like I'm swimming through molasses.

A voice says, "He's dead. I checked. He doesn't have a pulse," followed by a loud shout, "The hell he doesn't!!" The voice sounds familiar. I look down. There's a hand taking a carotid pulse. I realize it's mine.

I reach down to lift the limp, tattered child. I pull him to my chest with my right hand and hug him firmly. Blood dribbles from his mouth. My breathing becomes labored. The molasses gets thicker. I put my hand on his back to hold him tighter.

My hand enters the massive hole in his back, caused by a gun shot, and sinks in to the forearm.

I start screaming for help. Everything becomes white. My screams and the child are the only things that exist in the cloudy whiteness.

Snap! I came back to reality and started to cry. Then I remembered where I was. On a call with Rescue 1, trying to save Adam, a young boy who rode his bicycle into the street in front of a car. When we arrived at the hospital, I gave the ER doctor an account of how we found Adam, conscious and crying, trapped under the front of the car. *Every couple of minutes I'd see the red car and the dead kid in the back*

seat start looping in front of me. My voice wouldn't
respond as I wanted it to. My hands began to shake. I
cried again.

When we returned to the station after Adam's call,
the Deputy Chief relieved me from my duty and sent
me home. I went directly to bed and slept fourteen
hours. When I woke, I wanted to go back to sleep, but
made myself get up. I felt tired all day. The following
day, I still had to drag myself out of bed. I didn't want
to do anything. I remember taking the day off because
I still couldn't face work. All I wanted to do was sleep.

It took me six weeks after Adam's call until I felt
strong enough to return to work. Six long weeks,
compounded with an uncontrollable shaking anytime I
heard sirens or saw a fire engine. One-and-a-half
months of uncontrollable crying, without warning and
for no apparent reason—forty-five days of fear, pain
and feeling helpless.

Finally, I sought help. I spoke with a therapist for
an hour every week. I talked about my flashbacks of
the shooting; I talked about my reaction; I even talked
about my fear of children, my social life (or lack,
thereof), and computers ... it didn't matter, I talked
about anything. For the first time since the shooting, I
just talked about *things*. I admitted to fears and
phobias. I cried if I had to.

But, mostly, I just let six years of hell out. A hell I had created myself by not talking about the boy. The boy who had been shot by his father and left to die in a pool of his own blood.

Talking with the therapist helped. I was able to return to work and deal with the calls professionally. Major accidents, illnesses, child abuse cases and neglected child calls. Through all of it, I kept my composure.

Occasionally I would digress—back to 1984 and the call that changed my life—little Joey's shooting.

It was my third year with the Fire Department. I was assigned to Rescue 1, the busiest paramedic rig in the city. At the time I was twenty-six, the *immortal age*, when you think you're invincible and on top of the world.

It was a Saturday. The sun was hot, the sky cloudless. We hadn't turned a wheel that day, and were just settling down for lunch when the dispatcher called for Engine 4, Rescue 1 and Rescue 2 to assist Rescue 3 with a shooting on Lenox Road.

I knew the address—one block from where I grew up. We wasted no time getting to the rig, and flew out of the station, taking corners on two wheels. We covered two miles in less than a minute, looking for signs of a shooting —and a red compact two-door car.

When we reached the scene, the lieutenant from Rescue 3 was inside the car on the front seat taking care of a female patient. His partner was outside the driver's door on the sidewalk attending to a male patient. That was when I heard the scream, "Get in the car!"

I began to get in the front seat when the lieutenant said, "No, get in the back." So I folded the seat forward. That's when I saw Joey—and smelled the blood.

Five-year-old Joey was lying on his back with his head tilted to the right. I can still see the heavy eyelids, halfway closed over his brown eyes. His straight black hair sitting on his forehead. The pool of blood clotting around his shoulders. This innocent young boy, an unintentional victim of gunfire, shot by his own father—who had missed when trying to kill the boy's mother.

I thought I felt a pulse. I reached down, pulled him to me, and stood up outside the car. As I turned around, calling for a stretcher, I felt my hand slide into the hole where his back had been. The rushing and roaring in my ears rose at a frenzied rate, and I suddenly didn't feel anything.

I seemed to be floating above my body, swinging around in a circle. The only thing I could see was me holding this child. I was yelling, "Get me a stretcher!

Get me an ambulance!" Everything else was white.
Suddenly, I could see again. The lieutenant from
Rescue 2 had his hand on my shoulder, and said, "The
ambulance is here—it's right over there."

I carried Joey to the ambulance. We placed him on
a backboard on the floor and started working on him,
trying to save his life. We should have been four
minutes from Ellis Hospital. We made it in two. They
worked on him for forty-five minutes, to no avail. I
went to the bathroom and cried.

Returning to the scene to help clean up, I realized
that from the site I could see the house where I grew
up. Neighbors I'd known for my entire life approached
me, asking what happened. My father came to the
scene.

I felt my life dissolve.

When I got back to the station, I went to the
bunkroom to lie down. I lay there, staring at the ceiling
until we got another call—about fourteen hours later. I
couldn't close my eyes. I couldn't talk to anyone. I
heard the Deputy Chief suggest that I go home, but I
knew I couldn't. There was no one at home.

I convinced myself that I could handle it. No problem. All I had to do was get out of bed, and I would be
on the road to recovery.

Yeah, right.

Critical Incident Stress Debriefing wasn't an option when I was faced with this heavily traumatic experience. Since that time, we've had CISD training, and know how to recognize problems as they occur. I could have been the poster child for CISD. I spent six years struggling to cope with life after Joey's death. Sleepless nights, excessive drinking, weight loss and short, unpredictable temperament.

When CISD was introduced, I attended the sixteen-hour CISD Team training class, and realized just how much I needed a debriefing after the shooting. But I didn't realize how much I needed CISD until the same problem manifested years later as flashbacks. When this happened, I was experienced enough to realize I needed help, and reached out to the Fire Department's EAP coordinator. If not for the help that Richard Nebolini arranged for me, I doubt that I could have continued my career, and perhaps, not even my life.

I still have some residual baggage from the shooting. I have a difficult time dealing with children, and I have the occasional full sensory nightmare. But now when something bothers me, I don't keep it bottled up. If I see someone else in a bad situation, I try and help. I'll listen any time someone needs an ear, and I'll do my best to keep someone else from falling into the same trap.

Kurt Siegel, Captain
Schenectady Fire Department
Schenectady, New York

The Pre-Cordial Thump

*Do what you can, with what you have, where
you are.*

Theodore Roosevelt

Editor's Note:

*During the early 1970s the paramedic program was
just beginning in Southern California. Bold young men
and women would leave their stable jobs as firefighters
to endure six months of intensive training to provide
paramedic service to their community. Although the last
twenty-five years have brought many technological
advancements to their profession nothing can replace
the spirit and ingenuity these pioneers brought to every
call for help. Some of the methods they used may seem
antiquated today but were, nonetheless, very effective.*

It was the third day of seminars sponsored by our company with another full day of lectures to follow. The day began with the normal breakfast meeting, a half-hour break at ten, more lecture and then lunch. I noticed my friend Paul looked a little pale. He was in his early fifties and one of the most outgoing and likable guys I knew. At lunch he seemed unusually quiet, so I asked him how he was holding up through the torturous lectures.

Normally my friend would have responded with a witty reply. Instead, he commented that he wasn't feeling all that well, "But I'll make it," he said with a forced smile.

We all filed back into the room, took our seats and got ready to take notes for the last conference lecture.

After about a half-hour Paul seemed restless. I whispered to him to see if he was doing all right. He smiled back and nodded. "I'm going to lay my head down for a minute," he whispered.

After a few minutes I heard Paul inhale very deeply and then exhale with a sigh or moan. He became very limp and motionless. I immediately tried to wake him with no success, and yelled for someone to call 911.

With the assistance of my colleagues, we moved chairs and tables and laid Paul on the floor.

Everyone was in a state of shock, waiting for someone else to do something. I remember thinking that someone must know what to do, so get over here and do it!

Just then the doors swung open and in walked the firemen. They had arrived so quickly I thought they must have been next door. They immediately went to work. One firefighter leaned over Paul, tilted his head back, and then appeared to listen for his breath. He then put his fingers on Paul's neck, checking for a pulse.

Simultaneously, the other firefighter set up an oxygen mask as the Captain talked on his hand-held radio.

"He's not breathing and has no pulse, let's start CPR," the firefighter helping Paul said.

Suddenly, the seriousness of the situation grasped the entire room. This stuffy little conference room instantly became cold and eerily quiet. Not a word was spoken as twenty or so of Paul's friends and colleagues stood around him watching the firefighters try to save his life.

Two additional firefighters arrived carrying more equipment and I heard the Captain tell his firefighters that the paramedics were here.

"One and two and three and four and five ... One and two and three and four and five ... ." The firefighters continued CPR. While one of the paramedics attached wire leads to Paul's chest, the other began preparing an I.V. bag and medications. He placed a tourniquet around Paul's upper arm and began looking for a vein to start an I.V. line.

Paramedic Jim Dibble looked at the heart monitor, which was now attached to Paul. "Stop CPR," he firmly told the firefighters.

Without the firefighters repeating the CPR cadence, the room became deathly quiet.

Dibble looked at the heart monitor with such intensity that all eyes were on him. Some of us began leaning to gain a better look at what he saw. Even the firefighters seemed baffled and curious at what Jim saw and leaned in for a better look.

Without taking his eyes off of the monitor, Jim put his left hand on his paramedic partner's shoulder and said, "If his heart does that again I'm going to hit him."

Still glaring at the heart monitor, Jim placed the closed fist of his right hand over Paul's chest. A few seconds later he hit Paul in the chest and watched the monitor for the results. Everyone, even the firefighters, looked at Jim for a reaction.

"He's got a rhythm, continue to resuscitate him," Jim said, grinning slightly.

I could see the relief on the firefighter's face, but knew by their actions that the emergency was not over.

"He took a breath!" the firefighter giving oxygen told Jim.

"Assist him," Jim commanded.

"He's breathing on his own!" the firefighter excitedly declared within a minute.

"Keep him on the oxygen," Jim reminded.

I couldn't believe it. I watched a miracle take place before my very eyes. I looked around at my friends and felt so much emotion going on inside of me that I felt out of breath and couldn't speak. By the looks of everyone around me they were feeling the same. Then I heard a moan or groan and immediately returned my eyes back to Paul. He was opening his eyes and beginning to move his arms. I felt such elation I had trouble standing still.

"What's his name?" Jim asked, looking up at the crowd.

"Paul, his name is Paul," I immediately yelled.

"Paul, can you hear me?"

Paul nodded. Jim got real close to Paul's face.

"Paul we are the paramedics, it looks like you may

have had a heart attack, we are going to take you to the hospital, do you understand me?" Jim said.

"Yes," Paul said, again nodding his head.

"Just relax, Paul," Jim said smiling, as he patted my friend on the shoulder, "We'll take good care of you." Jim, showing great relief, looked up and told his partner that Paul was conscious, coherent, and speaking.

The room instantly exploded in applause. The feeling of amazement, joy and gratitude was overwhelming. Tears flowed and everyone hugged everyone. There was so much chatter we barely noticed the arrival of the ambulance, and Paul being carried off to the hospital.

My friend Paul walked out of the hospital a week later with his wife and three children at his side.

Thank you, Jim Dibble, and thanks to all firefighters and paramedics for your dedication and uncompromising duty to your communities.

Editor's Note:

The technique Paramedic Jim Dibble used when he hit Paul was a Pre-Cordial Thump. Because the defibrillator units in those days took so much time to set up, they were taught to use this technique to shock the heart into a normal rhythm in certain situations. This was the first and only time Paramedic Jim Dibble utilized the Pre-Cordial Thump in his twenty-year career as a paramedic.

As told to Curt Yoder

Nightmare in Oklahoma City

*I will seek that which was lost, and bring again
that which was driven away, and will bind up
that which was broken, and will strengthen that
which was sick.*

Ezekiel 34:16

We were sitting in the station house when the place
was rocked by what sounded like a thunderous
sonic boom. *No way*, I thought. *That was too powerful.*

I ran outside and saw a big cloud of smoke coming
from downtown. "Something bad's happened," I announced, not even bothering to be officially dispatched. "Let's go."

Two minutes later, we were dodging chunks of
debris, wire, and broken glass in the street. Parked
cars were burning and exploding all around us, their
tires bursting like bombs. *This is just too weird*, I
thought. It was like we had entered some futuristic,
post-nuclear holocaust scene.

As we approached the source of the smoke, the Alfred P. Murrah Federal Building, the debris on the street became so thick we couldn't differentiate between the road and the shoulder.

The instant we stopped, twenty-five people rushed toward us. Most were splotched with blood. Virtually all were screaming, crying, and pleading for help. We tried to organize the mob, and ourselves, as best we could, determining which ones were hurt the worst and treating them first. The others were told to be patient.

Some of the people who continued to pour out of the building were frantic; others were dazed. Those who could talk weren't making much sense. Everyone made reference to some kind of explosion, but no one had a clue what specifically had happened.

At some point I managed to glance up. Suddenly all the screaming and clamoring for help faded into the background, and my mind and body grew numb. Half the building was gone! "There's going to be a lot of dead people," I mumbled.

Turning away to shield my eyes from the harrowing sight, I spotted a soldier in uniform sprawled on the sidewalk. Another soldier was standing over him, trying to help. I walked over to see what was wrong.

"My arm's broken," the soldier said. "My back hurts."

I bent down to assess his injuries. Aside from his arm and back, he had a big, bloody gash on his head.

"You're going to be all right," I said. "Just wait here and we'll get you some help."

By that time, additional emergency units began to arrive. The situation outside appeared to be stabilizing. The survivors who made it that far generally had nonfatal cuts and burns. It was obvious that the people who were trapped inside needed our help the most.

We returned to our truck to prepare for the next phase of the rescue operation. That's when we made a critical discovery. The driveshaft of the Ryder van that we later learned held the terrorist bomb was on the ground next to us. "It was a car bomb," my partner, Don Carter, correctly surmised, waving over some federal agents.

The criminal investigation wasn't my concern. I grabbed my kit and headed toward the building's garage. The sprinkler system had ignited and was operating with a vengeance. I peered through the eerie mist and spotted a woman thrashing about in the puddles and wet debris. She was frantically trying to free herself from the chunks of concrete crushing her legs.

As I eased through the indoor rainstorm, I discovered three other bodies, all squashed beyond recognition. I shuddered, then moved deeper into the abyss. I was scared to death. There was stuff—big, heavy stuff—falling all around me in every direction, splashing violently into the pooled water. The whole structure creaked and cracked like the building was about to crumble any second.

I ignored my fear and pressed forward, finally reaching the woman. She had a severe head injury and was delirious and combative. I quickly realized that there was no way I could lift the heavy concrete slabs off her legs. I ran back outside to get help. The firefighters hadn't arrived yet, so I recruited the first person I saw, a man in his mid-thirties who was just standing around gawking.

"There's a lady trapped in there!" I choked, nearly out of breath. "I can't get her out. I need help! But it's dangerous—the debris is still falling. You'd be risking your life to help me."

"Let's do it," he said.

We charged back in and managed to get the woman free. That only made her scream and thrash around even more. I wrestled her to a backboard and, together with the good Samaritan, carried her to an ambulance. They transported her to the hospital alive, but she died in surgery.

Outside, I reunited with Don just as a firefighter handed him a baby. The firefighter, Chris Fields, and the baby, Baylee Almon, would later be pictured in newspapers around the world. Don took the child, and we both grimaced in horror. Her skull was cracked like an egg. There was nothing we could do.

Don had twins of his own, and holding this infant devastated him. I knew I had to get her away from him, get her away from everybody. Anyone who saw her would be horrified. I took the child in my arms and walked a block to the triage center.

"Mike, I have a dead baby here," I explained to my supervisor, Mike Murphy. "I don't want to leave her just anywhere."

"That truck's not leaving," he said, pointing to an ambulance being used as a supply center. "Put her there."

I gently wrapped the baby in a sheet and placed her in the back of the vehicle.

"God loves you," I whispered as the tears fell from my eyes. "God will look after you now."

As I walked back toward the ruins, I overheard someone say that there was a day care center in the building.

Oh, God, more children, I thought.

A police officer frantically waved me over.

"There's a guy alive up there on the third floor!"

I focused my eyes on where he was pointing. Sure enough, there was a man calmly sitting on the shattered edge of what had once been a floor. He could have been fishing, for all the emotion he showed.

The police constructed a makeshift ladder out of broken fence and slapped it against the building's jagged edges. Don and I climbed up. When we reached the man, we discovered why he was so calm. He was dead! His right leg had been torn off, his left leg was pinned under him, and the back of his head was sheared away. I have no idea what was holding him up like that. We covered him with a sheet, so that nobody else would think he was alive, and left him there to be dealt with later.

We proceeded to search through the rest of the floor for survivors but couldn't find any.

By then, the firefighters had tunneled their way to the day care center. That's when the real horror began. The firefighters dug the children out, one by one, and handed their broken bodies to us. Some of the kids had their clothes ripped right off them. Others were perfectly intact. The massive concussion from the bomb had simply blown out their lungs. It was pretty horrific. Each time I held another dead baby, it just tore my heart out.

Our misery was interrupted by more misery—a bomb scare. We were told that we were standing on a huge practice bomb owned by the Bureau of Alcohol, Tobacco, and Firearms and that we had to evacuate the building. Some of us thought that it was untrue and refused to leave. The rumor spread that the FBI just wanted time to investigate the crime scene and was using the alleged bomb as a ruse to clear everyone out.

Whatever the truth, we were forced to abandon our rescue efforts for nearly two hours at the most critical juncture. I sneaked back in a couple of times, desperate to search for any child that might need help, but was shooed away each time.

"If you go in one more time, Jana, I'm going to pull you from the scene," a supervisor scolded.

"But there are people dying who need us!" I protested.

"I know, but I don't want you to be one of them."

The long wait, combined with the ghastly images drained Don and me of what little energy we had left. I was soaking wet from the sprinklers, filthy, covered with blood, and totally exhausted, both physically and mentally. As it turned out, neither of us ever entered the building again.

I've since undergone extensive Critical Incident Stress Debriefing. And I've cried. Boy, have I cried. To this day, when I drive to work, I start crying. I keep asking myself, *Why? Why did this happen? Why the babies? Why here in Oklahoma City?* It just doesn't make sense. I can understand a natural disaster, but a mass murder like this?

I've had constant nightmares since that morning. In my dreams, I keep seeing those dead babies covered with white plasterboard dust. They look like ghosts. Hard as I try, though, I can't get to them.

It's been tough, but I don't think I'll quit being a paramedic. I plan to keep working. We've all received a lot of support from each other. I think that if we stick together, if we keep talking about it and don't clam up and let it eat at us, we'll be all right.

We'll never forget it, though. Never.

Jana Knox, Paramedic
Oklahoma City, Oklahoma
As told in Angels of Emergency
by Donna Theisen and Dary Matera

They Emerged from the Smoke

*To let oneself be bound by a duty from the
moment you see it approaching is part of the
integrity that alone justifies responsibility.*

Dag Hammarskjold

Firefighters throughout the western United States
will always remember the *Fire Storms of 1993*.

An especially warm summer and ensuing drought
left most of California's wildland areas dry and brittle.
Exactly one week after the Laguna Beach firestorm
ravaged its seaside community, the Malibu fire
erupted. I was a newly promoted Battalion Chief
assigned to our department's Fire Operations when
this second of three major fires hit California.

On the second day of the Malibu firestorm, I was
dispatched to lead a strike team from Orange County
to support the massive efforts to stop this conflagra-
tion. It was my first test as the commanding officer of

a strike team during one of the most memorable firefights I can remember.

I met with five engine companies from our surrounding area in an Orange County shopping center parking lot. There we planned our route and established our radio travel channel. We were instructed to report to "Pepperdine Command" which I figured was a staging area near the fire. The two and a half hour drive north from Orange County to Malibu seemed to last forever. Each mile we traveled brought us closer to the massive smoke column that ascended thousands of feet into the air.

When dispatched to urban/wildland interface fires out of our area, there is always a chance of being sidelined as reserve manpower and being forced to watch the firefight from staging areas or surrounding fire stations—on television. As we advanced upon the growing tower of smoke, it seemed to all of us we would be getting right into action because of the magnitude of this fire.

As our firefighting convoy drew closer to the fire area we noticed the off ramp to our assigned destination was past Malibu—past the main body of the fire. My heart sank as I checked with dispatch to re-verify our destination. Dispatch confirmed our original instruction—we were to continue past the fire area.

When we arrived at the "last outpost" fire station, I instructed my strike team to refuel their rigs and stand by while I reported in. The Captains followed me into the office where we were greeted with, "Thank God you are here. I need your five engines to fill empty fire stations." The Captains from my strike team gathered around the office door and looked at me with a *say-it-ain't-so* expression on their faces.

"There must have been some sort of mix-up," I suggested to my men. I instructed the Captains to feed their crews and go on stand-by while I worked this out. As my small army of officers left the room I felt like I had let them down. We came so far only to sit in various fire stations watching the battle on fire station televisions. Still determined to get in the fight, I contacted the Pepperdine staging officer who told me that we had been sent to the wrong location. I was told to report to Pacific Coast Highway (PCH) staging.

From my Suburban radio, I announced the new assignment to my strike team. The cheer was deafening. I instructed them to follow me Code-3 to Malibu.

We arrived at the PCH staging area around ten o'clock that night. We were assigned to protect a grocery store and neighboring motel, which consisted of ten small bungalow-style buildings. Leaving our rigs on PCH we advanced hand lines between the bungalows. In front of us was a shallow wash with twelve- to fifteen-foot tall bamboo thickets. Beyond the bamboo was a hillside that rose to a height of three hundred feet. The Division Group Supervisor told us that strong winds were pushing the fire in our direction, and we were to stop it before it reached the motel and store. The strike team took their positions, with hose lines and battle equipment ready. I positioned myself in an area that provided a good vantage point to see my crew and observe the advancing fire front. When the wall of fire crested the ridge—night seemed to turn into day. The wind blew thirty miles per hour, plus, and brought the heat from the flames uncomfortably close. The temperature rose considerably.

As the heat intensified, I was overwhelmed by the sense of awesome responsibility—the responsibility I had to protect my crew. The danger of the situation was immense. While these brave firefighters gave me the thumbs-up to continue, I realized that even in the gravest situation they wouldn't make the personal decision to walk away from the job they came to do—or walk away from their fellow brothers and sisters. They came to fight this fire and depended on me to take care of the rest. These firefighters and their families were counting on me to make the decisions that would bring them home safely.

I met with each crew and made sure everyone had all of their protective gear in place. I told each Captain that I had selected an area of refuge in front of the grocery store, and pointed out the escape routes to be used if the fire forced them to withdraw from their current positions.

As the fire advanced rapidly toward our position, we were pelted with flaming firebrands and hot ash.

Again I checked my crews, monitored their positions and asked if they were doing okay.

"We're doing great, Chief," they replied.

The wind-driven fire made its way to the bamboo, which exploded into flames like a torch. The fire front grew at an alarming rate. Flames soared seventy-five feet into the black sky. Our hose streams were directed into the advancing threat with little effect. Spot fires began to form behind the front lines and the smoke was suffocating. I checked my crews one more time and, again, a thumbs-up was their response.

I will never forget the feeling of helplessness that swept over me when I saw flames devouring the hose streams without hesitation. The howling wind sounded like a freight train and the smoke became so thick I lost sight of my men. We were facing a real firestorm and didn't have the manpower to stop it. My men were overwhelmed and in an instant it became a life or death situation.

I swiftly started toward the front line to get my men out. Hearing something behind me, I turned to see what seemed like images at first, steely-eyed, lantern-jawed, soot-covered firefighters emerging from the smoke and advancing hose lines to support my men.

This army of firefighters was everywhere. The streams they added to the battle began to immediately affect the wall of flames. I watched in disbelief as these phantom firefighters advanced their lines until they were shoulder to shoulder with my men. We were gaining the upper hand. I remember thinking *if we only had chopper support,* although I knew helicopters, as a rule, don't fly at night. Suddenly over the roar of the flames I heard a familiar sound. Looking over my shoulder I saw the most beautiful white and red helicopter approaching us from the west. I watched as it banked right and delivered its payload of water with pinpoint accuracy. The firefighters responded with a roaring cheer. Another drop was made a few moments later and the Huey disappeared over the hilltop. We had beaten this fire.

As the sun began to brighten the morning sky, I watched as these firefighters, these comrades, shook hands, hugged and patted each other on the back. It was truly a night we would never forget. I shook hands with my fellow Battalion Chief and thanked him for his timely arrival. He explained they were a roving strike team, sent to help us against the advancing wall of fire.

We were successful in our mission. Each brave firefighter returned home to their family without injury. The store and motel sustained only minor damage. Later that morning relief personnel began to arrive. As each crewmember was relieved, I thanked them personally for their outstanding efforts.

Driving home, I reflected on the events of the night and thanked God for His divine intervention by sending us these brave firefighters that *emerged from the smoke.*

James M. Ellis, Battalion Chief
Costa Mesa Fire Department
Costa Mesa, California

Once Upon A Time

*The greatest discovery of my generation is that
man can alter his life simply by altering his
attitude of mind.*

James Truslow Adams (1878-1949)

Three of us sat on the back step of Engine 1 sipping
water and making vain attempts at clearing soot
from our sinuses. We were two hours into the fire and
just starting to gain ground when we'd been pulled out
for a mandatory breather. We were all *call men* on that
step, each of us with families and lives we'd run out on
when the radio called. There were full timers, both on
duty and off, working right alongside us. The Duty
Captain stood by the myriad of knobs, which controlled our weapon, our water. Above the roaring
flames I heard someone talk with the Captain and his
words brought me to my feet. I dragged my sodden

form to where the two of them stood, My colleagues followed, curious of my abrupt departure.

The firefighter, a full timer, was complaining that his shift had been up forty-five minutes ago. He wanted to leave. I shook my head as the argument drew to an end. I know the aggravation faced by those who work in the station. Unions. Bureaucracy. Politics. It wears down the heartiest of souls. But still.

The argument lost, the firefighter had taken barely three steps when I spoke. I faced the Captain but no one had to guess whom I addressed.

"You know, Cap, I knew this guy once, a call man. Hell of a guy. Funny? The man could make you laugh in the middle of a flashover. Serious though, knew what it was about. Didn't play games when it mattered. Watched your back, too. I remember him pulling me back more than once and telling me to look. I don't recall anyone loving what he did more than him. Man, when that tone went out I know I sure as hell didn't want to be in his way! He'd be in his glory on a night like this. He worked his way to full time, didn't he, Cap? Hey, you haven't seen him, have you?"

He had turned to face us in mid stalk. Our eyes met as I spoke the last sentence directly to him. His already flushed face deepened several shades and his muscles tensed. I may have overstepped my boundaries, but I held my ground as he took slow, measured steps toward me. He stopped inches away and I braced for a beating. His eyes never left mine; his gloved hand came to rest on my shoulder.

"Yeah," he said, the crooked grin I remembered so well brightening his face, "I think I know right where he is. Want to fight a fire with him?"

Michael R. Chase, Firefighter/EMT
Nantucket Fire Department
Nantucket, Massachusetts

Those Who Forever Touch Our Hearts

Memorable Moments that Forever
Tie Our Hearts to Those We Serve

What Was Her Name?

*How deceitful hope may be, yet she carries us
on pleasantly to the end of life.*

Duc de La Rouchefoucauld

I awoke before dawn and was dispatched to an
isolated section of road down by the river in
Evansville, Indiana. We were informed by dispatch of a
possible vehicle into a telephone pole with two seri-
ously injured victims.

When we arrived, light had just begun to envelop
the sky, but the vast, open area around us remained
dark and quiet. The front of the truck was crushed
head on into a telephone pole, leaving power lines
draped over the remains of the vehicle's crumpled
hood. A man, apparently electrocuted, lay on the
ground near the passenger side door. A critically

injured woman, still conscious, but bleeding from a
gash on her head, was slumped to one side in the
passenger seat. There was broken glass and torn metal
scattered everywhere.

It was apparent the driver got out of the truck and
went over to the passenger's door to assist the young
woman after the accident. When he opened the door to
assist the girl, the still-live power line must have
surged and electrocuted him, killing him instantly.

The passenger, clinging to life, remained there until
a passing car spotted them and called 911.

After quickly moving the electrical line out of the
way, one crew began immediately trying to revive the
male patient, while my crew concentrated on the
female patient. As I moved around her and assisted
with setting up the I.V. and stabilizing procedures, I
noticed she was watching my every move. I talked to
her continuously, gently explaining what was going on,
but she was unable to verbally respond. The whole
time she never looked away from me.

The helicopter soon arrived to transport her to the
hospital. We loaded her onto the helicopter and I
watched it take off. I couldn't help but feel a bond with
this stranger and a deep concern for her well being.
After the helicopter left, we remained at the site to help

clean up debris and complete the necessary paper-work.

What I heard next filled me with profound shock and sorrow. As the Sheriff read off the young woman's name from her driver's license, I was stunned. My mind flashed back to the familiar face of a dear friend from high school. This was not a stranger, but a classmate I joked around with and, together, studied and copied off each other's papers. Although our paths led us in different directions, we had remained friends.

I suddenly realized that the reason she followed me everywhere with her eyes was because *she* recognized *me*. She must have been looking for a sign that I recognized her, but I never gave her that. Her injuries were too severe. The wooded area too dark to tell that she was a special friend.

In a flash, it all came flooding through my head. Every time I had ever talked with her, worked with her in class to get the right answer, her smile and her laugh—I remembered.

My regret and sorrow intensified. Later, I learned that she had died as a result of her injuries. I began asking myself: *Why couldn't I have recognized her? Why couldn't I have at least been able to reassure her that I knew who she was? Why couldn't I give her hope?*

These thoughts haunted me for quite some time. Until I finally realized that I had done everything I could for her. It was something that was in her fate, and nobody could change that.

Through this experience I have become a different person. I no longer work around my patients as though they are inanimate objects. Since that day, I have made it a point to develop a bond with my patients. I either ask them, or find out from someone, their first name, and through my entire interaction with them, use their name repeatedly. I let my patient know who I am. I want them to know that I, and everyone at that scene, are doing everything we can for them and that they have to do their part and stay strong.

I have decided that putting a patient on a cot is not enough for me. I want to have that patient know that I care.

Some people tell me it isn't healthy to give emotionally, or create a bond with a patient. But I know they are wrong. Wrong in a big way.

I know that no matter what, whether the patient lives or, regretfully, dies, I gave them hope. My life has brought me riches beyond belief for doing this. Yes, I have lost some of these new friends to injuries and illnesses that I couldn't help or stop. But I sleep well knowing that their final seconds on earth were ones of love and hope.

Gary Barr, Firefighter
Evansville, Indiana

Same Old Story

God asks no man whether he will accept life.
That is not the choice. You must take it. The only
question is how.

Henry Ward Beecher

My partner and I were having a day you always
dread. Although it was a beautiful, warm summer day, we were so busy we hadn't had a chance to
enjoy a minute. The Emergency Room was a mess, and
every time we came back in to restock we were dispatched to another call.

One call led to another and, while we were still
discussing what we should eat for lunch, it was
suppertime. As we stood at the doors of the ER decid-
ing whether we should go get some food, or just wait
another hour until our shift was over, we were dispatched to a man in respiratory distress. As we rushed

to the ambulance, my partner said, "Well, at least this will be our last call because when we get back from this, our relief will be there." I laughed and agreed, then radioed dispatch for better directions.

We arrived on scene. We approached the house and were met at the door by an elderly woman—the man's wife. She quickly led us to him, and explained to us that her husband had a heart condition and had several heart attacks in the past. Today had been a good day for him and he had felt better than he normally did, however, over the past hour had become short of breath and wasn't at all acting like himself.

We found him sitting in a chair. At first glance I knew he was in dire need of medical attention. He was obviously suffering from a catastrophic cardiac event that had caused his heart to slow to a rate in the twenties, and he appeared to be in shock.

While we worked on him, she told us that they had an enjoyable time when visited earlier that day by their niece, whom they hadn't seen in several years. She also expressed deep concern about his failing medical condition, which prevented him from planting a garden—the first time in fifty years. She seemed very calm and, at one time, asked why we were working so quickly. As we loaded him in the ambulance and prepared him for transport, I asked her if she had a ride to the hospital and she stated she would meet us there.

Upon arrival at the hospital he was feeling better. We had done considerable intervention, most of which was only temporary. I felt his chance of recovery was poor, at best. His wife met us at the hospital and thanked us for our quick response. We directed her to the waiting area.

After evaluation, and more intervention at the hospital, his family physician was consulted. It was concluded that the wife would have to decide whether she wanted life support continued, or not. She talked with the doctor for several minutes. She expressed that she knew her husband wouldn't want to live the rest of his life in this condition. He had been an active individual his entire life, and to see him this way was more than she could bear. Upon her request, she was brought to his room so she could speak to him and see if he would help her with this heart wrenching decision.

Their conversation was brief.

They began to say good-bye.

He was in considerable discomfort and he seemed very willing to leave this life for whatever eternity had in store. He appeared fearless and decisive. As the

I.V.s and electronic equipment that kept his heart beating were discontinued, he closed his eyes.

I could feel a large lump in my throat as he took his last breath, while his wife of fifty years held his hand in hers, and quietly wept. I felt as though they had to be the most courageous couple I had ever met. Although my encounter with them was brief, it impacted me as though we had been friends forever.

At that moment, I suddenly realized all I had learned about my profession and all the experience I had gained meant nothing compared to the lesson I had just learned. I prayed that when it was my turn to leave this life, as I knew it, I could be as brave and as absolute about the decision as they were.

I left the hospital that night knowing in my heart that my profession was more than just a job. I knew destiny played a role in every person's life and felt as though this may have been the reason I was traveling on this road and wondered if I was taking the right path. I had realized a different ending to the same old story and, although it wasn't the ending I would have chosen when the call began, it was one that was worthy of thought.

As I left the hospital parking lot and headed west, toward home, I could see as always, the sun setting on the horizon. I was glad the sky was cloudless and thought of how often I had seen the sun set as I drove home. That same horizon held many sunsets, each one different than the last and, by its own right, an individual masterpiece of nature never to be duplicated and—when darkness fell—gone forever. Tonight would be no exception—and it was beautiful.

While driving, I realized there was always a different ending to the same old story, though I never took notice. Tonight I discovered what had been in my grasp all along. Never again will I search for answers in far away places, until I have exploited the simple things.

W. J. Wilde, Paramedic
Pennsylvania

Gone, But Never Forgotten

*Holding the heart of another in the comforting
hands of prayer is a priceless act of love.*

Janet L. Weaver

On May 3, 1999, while working an extra shift at the
fire department in downtown Costa Mesa, California, our paramedic engine was dispatched to a reported vehicle accident. I was the Captain on the
Quint, which is a combination fire engine and truck
company. Shortly after the paramedic engine was
dispatched, I heard on the radio that this call might
involve a car into a pre-school yard. We were dispatched to "reported children trapped under a vehicle."
Seeing small children suffer is every firefighter's
nightmare.

We responded and I could tell by the voices of
those already on-scene that this was a serious call. I

told my guys that we would use the air bags to lift the car off the children. Moments later we were on-scene. What I saw was indescribable. A large older-model Cadillac had plowed through a chain-link fence and was up against a large tree. Some small children were lying on the ground around the car, while the uninjured were being led away from the gruesome site. The playground's swing-set lay mangled, the driver's target. At least twenty concerned citizens were around the car and had already lifted the car enough to remove the two previously trapped children. Because of their efforts, our air bags were not needed.

Citizens and firefighters worked together to help the other children. The eyes and faces of those present were filled with horror, sorrow, and helplessness. You see, only moments earlier, this pre-school schoolyard was full of tiny innocent children laughing and playing. Their lives were simple and full of fun. Now they were full of fear, crying at all the unwanted attention.

Numerous children and one teacher were injured. However, God had other plans for the two children trapped under the car. Sierra was killed instantly. As soon as she was pulled from under the car, her four-year-old body was covered with a blanket. Brandon was unconscious and barely breathing. His mother, who had come to the school to take him home, was devastated. The paramedics quickly transported three-year-old Brandon to the Emergency Room where a crew of doctors and nurses awaited his arrival. Even with the most aggressive efforts by the paramedics and hospital staff, this happy little boy who loved his stuffed bear and loved to help clean the house, could not be saved.

My crew split up to assess and assist those injured. I first went to the aid of five-year-old Victoria. She was lying in the sand a few feet from the front wheel on the passenger side of the car. A lady was holding her hand. I spoke to Victoria calmly and smiled as I asked her simple questions while checking her for injuries. She had sand in her clothes and hair, and her face was slightly bloodied. She was being so brave, especially for having a skull and pelvis fracture. Her mother arrived, and I did my best to keep her calm as I turned the care of Victoria over to the paramedics for transportation to a trauma center.

Once the others injured were being treated, I went into the courtyard to see if any further assistance was needed. This is where I heard Cindy, Sierra's mother, cry out as she received news of her daughter, her only child. Someone assisted her into one of the classrooms where a Trauma Intervention Member tried to comfort her. Seeing this caused my heart to ache. As I left the courtyard to go back to the play area, I looked at the tiny covered body of Sierra. An inner voice told me that this is where I was needed. I went over to her and kneeled beside her. Even though she was now with the Lord, I felt I had to sit with her. If this were my child, I wouldn't want him to be alone. So I sat. The Battalion Chief asked me to confirm if this was a boy or a girl. It was then that I discreetly lifted the blanket and met Sierra for the first time.

This call was bad enough, but what I heard next just made me sick. I discovered that the driver of the vehicle, who continued to sit in the car, admitted to deliberately driving his car onto the playground to hit these children. His heart seemed unmoved by the death and pain he had brought to these children and their families. He was upset about a failed relation-ship, and after seeing the children laughing and playing, decided to *execute innocent children.* He turned his car around and stepped on the gas as he headed for the playground. Yes, he calmly admitted that he did this deliberately.

While I sat with Sierra, praying for God to take care of her, and letting her know we would look after her mother, the news of this intentional act made me both angry and more emotionally upset. I had thought that this was an accident due to a medical problem, or perhaps a mechanical problem. I could not, and still can't, comprehend how any human could intentionally run down sweet, loving children.

Since the accident, my wife and I have become good friends with Sierra's mother and I have a beautiful picture of Sierra in my locker at work. I truly believe that I was meant to be on this call. Even though I never knew Sierra in life, I have grown to love her and think of her often. I think her death was instrumental in my becoming a real Christian. Sierra's mother, Cindy, recommended a series of Christian books, which have helped my wife and me to spread the faith and continue to learn God's word. I believe God wanted me to be there for Sierra's mother. Cindy told me she appreciated my treating Sierra like a person by sitting with her lifeless little body when she was emotionally devastated and unable to be there for her. She has shared with me that my conversations with her have brought comfort.

Cindy started a foundation in memory of her daughter. *Sierra's Light Foundation* is a foundation to help make schools safer for our children. God is using this tragedy to touch souls and to give special meaning to the shortened lives of these two precious children. Evil will not triumph!

Even though I have seen many sad and unfortunate things happen in my twenty-two years in the fire service, the thought of Brandon's and Sierra's deaths continues to weigh heavily on my heart. Because of the callous nature, and my involvement during the call, I have an emotional bond never felt before. Besides my own personal growth, I feel as though the Lord wants me to use this tragedy to reach others. I continue to pray for guidance.

Even though she was only four years old, Sierra was already an accomplished dancer. Just days before she was killed, Sierra won first place at a dance competition. I never had the opportunity to see her perform. However, I know she is dancing for God now and I look forward to seeing her dance for me someday. Until we meet again, my thoughts are with you often, Sierra. I love you.

Gregg A. Steward, Captain
Costa Mesa Fire Department
Costa Mesa, California

Small World

There is a magnet in your heart that will attract true friends. That magnet is unselfishness, thinking of others first ... when you learn to live for others, they will live for you.

Paramahansa Yogananda

Yet another quiet Sunday, hot and humid, laying on the deck playfully spraying my giggling daughter with the hose. The weekend had been busy, extraordinarily so, and why I thought Sunday would be different, I had no idea.

I heard the tone from the living room radio and, knowing a first rescue was already out, headed for my portable telephone. I was first to call in, but living closer to the scene than the station, I was told to respond direct. Shoes on, I fired up the truck and was on scene within four minutes.

Waved in to an obscure driveway, I parked the truck and radioed the rescue with precise directions.

Several people were kneeling next to a fallen woman in the middle of a horse arena. As I approached, bystanders informed me she'd been thrown from her horse. She didn't strike her head, but had lost consciousness for several minutes. Seeing no bleeding, I immediately took cervical traction and opened a dialogue. She was alert and oriented, but had no recollection of the incident or the minutes before. She claimed no head pain, only tenderness to her left knee.

Rescue 3 arrived, complete with another Emergency Medical Technician and driver. We swiftly went to work. Within three minutes she was collared, boarded and on the cot in the ambulance, where we obtained vitals and pertinent information for the hospital. We immediately got under way. The other EMT handled the radio as I applied ice packs and worked to keep my nervous charge as calm as possible. Working with what I know, I drew on my lifelong experience with horses and opened a conversation. Then I learned what a small world it really is.

I was telling her of a young Arabian I'd had several years previous, the last horse my wife and I had before she passed away. I had to give him up for financial and personal reasons. She began asking me about the animal, distinguishing marks, habits, training, and his name. As fate would have it, her son now owned my horse. I was near speechless, thinking Lucky Seven had been taken off the island, and barely found the strength to ask how he was. The rest of the way to the hospital she told me what a marvelous animal he was, and how much her son loved him. Our arrival came far too quickly.

Following the usual routine, we settled our patient and began refitting the rig. I, being first on scene, received the honor of doing the paperwork. I finished up and went first to the exam room to wish her good luck, then to the waiting room to reassure her waiting husband and children she would be alright. Her husband was just getting off the phone as I entered and I let them know what to expect, and that she was getting the best of care. We said goodbye and I headed out to the rescue for the ride back to my truck. The drive passed quickly with thoughts and memories of something and someone I truly missed.

I was walking from the rig to my truck, head lowered in concentration, when a voice called to me from the barn. The owner called me to ask if I knew how her friend was getting along. It led into more casual conversation. As I enjoyed the conversation, I heard a horse being led in to the alley behind me, nothing out of the ordinary in a barn. The owner's grin, however, told me I should probably look. I turned, and my breath caught. I could feel my nose stinging with pending tears. Memories both bitter and sweet came to me when I saw Lucky Seven in full gear. My patient had her husband call the barn and request that he be saddled for me when I picked up the truck. I spent a wonderful afternoon getting reacquainted with an old friend.

I also was given a telephone number with a message to feel free to ride old Lucky Seven as often as I wished.

What a small world it is.

Michael R. Chase, Firefighter/EMT
Nantucket Fire Department
Nantucket, Massachusetts

A Legend in Their Own Time

Friendship is the golden thread that ties the
hearts of all hearts of all the world.

John Evelyn

M any communities have someone that you see
every time you pass a certain house on that
street. You may know them by name, even stop and
converse with them on occasion. Our small rural
village of Alexandria, Ohio, was blessed enough to
have two such individuals: a husband and wife.

This older married couple lived just three houses
from the firehouse, on the only major thoroughfare
through town. The people who passed their home on
the way to and from the firehouse were always greeted
by either one or both of them. Members of the department would frequently stop and chat with them. It
didn't matter if you were new, or had been around for

decades, they treated you like they'd known you for years. They treated members of the community like their family, and strangers like long lost friends. When visiting the firehouse my two young sons delighted in stopping by to visit this special, loving couple as much as playing on the fire engines.

The village our fire department protects is a town with many older, heavy timber buildings constructed at the inception of the town—sometime in the 1800s. This special couple, we'd all grown fond of, ran a business out of their home constructed of heavy timber, with a brick exterior. We knew the wood was well seasoned, like most of the older homes in the area, and that if a fire ever occurred, it would be a real battle.

Our fire department hosted a class one evening in early February. We completed class for the evening and headed out around eleven o'clock. My car was parked in front of their house. The elderly gentleman was sitting outside, which was not uncommon for him at this time of night. I bid him goodnight, left for home and went to bed.

My pager went off at one-thirty in the morning for a reported structure fire, called in by a passing motorist. The address given was that of the elderly couple's home. My husband, who is also a firefighter, was up, dressed and gone before I could get a babysitter for our two sons. I prayed that the motorist had just seen the flickering of the television set and mistaken it for a fire.

A firefighter who lived just down the street answered county dispatch. He confirmed a working fire.

I arrived on the fire scene approximately ten minutes after the first engine. We received mutual aid from surrounding departments and an aggressive entry was attempted, but the firefighters were pushed back by the fire and the threat of a possible collapse. The offensive attack was forced into a defensive posture. As I was donning my gear, a member of the squad crew came up to me and asked if I knew where the couple was. I said no, and hurried to the scene commander. I saw the couple's car parked outside the house, but no sign of them. I hoped that someone had taken them to the firehouse and was giving them a warm cup of coffee and a blanket.

We continued until sunrise to extinguish the fire, trying to limit the extension. Access was denied into the building pending closer examination for signs of collapse. Sometime during the night, the determination was made that neither one of the couple had escaped the flames. This proved difficult for the members of the community who stood ... and watched ...

anxious for some word, some sign of hope. For a fire department, any loss of life is devastating, but for our small town there would be an extra blow—several of the firefighters were relatives of this couple.

When the fire was extinguished we began sifting through the charred rubble, looking for remains near a burned away exterior wall, where the man often slept. I had never been on a call to a fatal fire. My heart stopped with each handful of belongings I lifted. A doll's melted hair ... a man's shirt ... cushions on a chair. They all began to feel and look like the bodies we were searching for. We wanted to find them to get them out, yet, hoped we wouldn't, and were scared with every step. We desperately hoped they had secretly gone on a trip with friends.

We gained approval to begin searching the upper floors. There was a very limited time frame because of the building's condition. A crew entered the second of three stories from the outside.

We heard nothing.

The first crew finally emerged without success. The decision was made to form a mutual aid company to attempt the second search.

Again, we waited.

From out of the window opening one of the crewmembers announced they had found her, and were going to continue the search for him. A few minutes later they came to the opening and said they had found him.

The State Fire Marshal's Office entered the building and completed the necessary tasks prior to the removal of the bodies. The body bags were somberly passed up the ladder—the couple placed in them. Each was handed down the ladder to a line of firefighters, who gently loaded them into the hearse.

We stayed throughout the day, assisting the Fire Marshal where necessary. At dusk, a backhoe was called in to demolish the building because of the threat of collapse onto the main road and parking lots. It was eerie and heartbreaking, to watch the backhoe knock down the house while silhouetted by the moon and streetlights, much as it looked when I said my final goodnight to our neighbor the evening before.

We later learned that they had died of smoke inhalation and, miraculously, suffered few burns. Somehow this was supposed to be consoling, but it wasn't.

They had died just feet from one another. The speculation was that they became disoriented as he was trying to help her out. I replayed the night of the fire in my mind, looking for some sign, some glow of what was to come. I often wish I had some sixth sense and could have warned him instead of saying my last goodnight to him that night.

The site of the fire has long since been cleared of debris. And the home that brought so many memories is now an empty lot surrounded by a wire fence that holds weathered plastic flowers, and a cross.

It is a stark reminder of what we fight every day to prevent.

Johneen "Jay" Castle, Firefighter/EMT
Alexandria—St. Albans Township Fire Department
Alexandria, Ohio

Five-Minute Break

*There is destiny that makes us brothers, none
goes his way alone. All that we send into the
lives of others comes back into our own.*
                                    Edwin Markham

The telltale vibration in my mask tells me it's time
to back out. The air in my breathing apparatus is
running low. I feel the hand of my backup man on my
shoulder, cut back the stream, and reluctantly hand
off the nozzle of my deuce-and-a-half. As I back down
the line, I see where the flames will break through the
wall next. This break will be a short one.

My hands are my eyes; my feet, my sense of direction as I follow the wall and the hose line out. Down
through the second floor, heat, ash and smoke drift on
the air in a promise. This fire wasn't ready to quit. The
air cools as I descend to the first floor, allowing another layer of ash to settle on my saturated bunkers

and face mask. The noon sun does little to help me pick my way though the tangle of lines and ladders, as I head toward the back engine. A button's push and a quarter turn release the regulator and I take in the first real air I've breathed in nearly an hour. Gloves soaked hit the step with a thud and my wrinkled fingers work to remove first the helmet, then the mask. I drop both to the ground and sit, momentarily blinded on the engine's step. Something is thrust in my hand—water. I drink deeply and rub the spots from my eyes.

My eyes focus, finally, and the cup stops half way to my parched mouth. My first clear vision shows me a man. He sits quietly on a bench just the other side of the fire tape. Unlike the other spectators a fire always draws, he is not pointing or gawking or whispering. He's not snapping pictures or killing time. He sits, hands folded in his lap, staring fixedly at the second floor of the burning building. My vision has cleared enough to see the tears falling from his unblinking eyes. I feel a stinging in the bridge of my nose and realize, suddenly, that I'm crying with him. The man is not watching some anonymous building burn. This is not just some business being gutted by flame. This man is watching the destruction of his home, his life, his memories—and he cries out with frustration and fear as I sit watching. He is powerless to alter the events unfolding before him ...

... but I am not.

A fresh bottle on my back, I plunge with fresh determination back into the inferno.

Michael Chase, Firefighter/EMT
Nantucket Fire Department
Nantucket, Massachusetts

On A Lighter Note

Stories We Like to Tell Over and Over Again ...

Yes, A Cat in the Tree

Out of intense complexities, intense simplicities emerge.

Winston Churchill

One afternoon, three of us were at the volunteer fire station doing paperwork from another call when the phone rang. It was a distraught male concerned about, believe it or not, a cat in the tree. I had always heard about fire departments making such calls, but I'd never seen one, and had never been involved in one.

The man said the cat had been up there for more than fifteen hours. It was a stray and was driving the family crazy with its loud, continuous meowing. He said he felt silly calling a fire department for a *cat in a tree* but to get the cat down he had tried all other resources he knew such as food and milk, with no

113

success. I suggested hurling a few small stones to scare it down, but he explained his daughter was an animal rights activist and wouldn't hear of any type of inhumane activity.

So, the three of us jumped in the engine and headed out.

We drove eight miles to the farthest reach of our district and sure enough found a cat in a tree, meowing like crazy and sounding scared and upset.

One of our volunteers had just gone through extensive high-angle rescue training, and was anxious to test out his newfound skills and wisdom. He volunteered to save the cat.

What took place for the next couple of hours was impressive and somewhat comical.

Our high-angle rescue expert took charge of the situation and had everybody doing something. We set up two straight ladders to create an A-frame above the cat with connected pulleys, caribiners, eight plates and a variety of stuff I never thought we'd use. There were ropes to hoist, ropes for safety, and even a rope attached to our rubbish carrier to be used as a basket to carry the cat down. Some ropes were attached to the fire truck as an anchor point, while other ropes were being tendered by us, the two remaining volunteer firefighters, and newly recruited neighbors. This was one major undertaking!

I was really impressed by what transpired, but kept thinking to myself: *Why doesn't somebody just climb the tree, grab the cat, and carry it down?*

About an hour and a half later, after checking everything thoroughly, the volunteer stepped into a harness with several ropes attached to it and began his ascent.

As he climbed the tree, the rope tenders were instructed to keep tension on the rope. Once he got into place, near the cat, they would hoist up the rescue basket in which he would gently place the cat. Together, they would be lowered to safety.

As he approached the cat I noticed that this cute little fur ball was getting very anxious. Its meowing had intensified to a monotone growl.

The firefighter positioned himself about a foot below the cat and secured his self into place. He was looking down motioning for the basket to be hoisted up when the cat decided that it had had about enough of this.

Our adventurous volunteer, and leader of this operation, became the ramp this cat needed. All of a sudden, the cat went into feline panic mode and all but attacked the man! Hair raised and claws extended, the cat launched itself onto the volunteer. Merely using the firefighter as traction, the cat quickly and abruptly jumped down to the ground! Seemingly unscathed, the cat scurried at breakneck pace off into the woods.

We were left standing there with enough equipment to impress the National Guard. We all had a great laugh. The homeowner, still feeling silly, was very grateful for our efforts and made a generous donation to our Fire Department. All in all, it was a worthwhile effort and we accomplished what we were called to do.

There was one valuable lesson learned that day. Regardless of how silly a situation may seem, we wouldn't be called unless someone needed our help. And that's what we're here for ... to help others.

Tim Miller, Assistant Chief
Saginaw Volunteer Fire and Rescue
Saginaw, Alabama

Where Is It?

The love of truth lies at the root of much humour.
Robertson Davies

We responded to a structure fire early one afternoon that was paged out of our district. Our station was about ten minutes from the fire, so our engine would arrive after the nearest station, only two minutes from the scene. As we got closer to the area, we were informed by dispatch that the closest station had not yet found the address.

Our district had just recently been added to the 911 system, so all the streets and addresses were new to us. Arriving in the neighborhood of the fire, we met up with the pumper engine of the other station. The driver of the other pumper had no idea where this house was, so we spread out to find it. As luck would have it, I followed the road I was on, which looped around. I found the house on the other side of the loop. I radioed the other station's pumper to tell them where we were, and we set up our engine to extinguish the fire.

Luckily, it was only a stove that had run amuck, and the house was undamaged. After turning the gas off and clearing some smoke from the kitchen area, I found the driver of the other pumper. He was standing in the driveway with his head hanging down. I asked him what was the matter.

He said with a grin, "I live right there!" His house was only about a hundred feet from the house that had made the call!

He took some ribbing for that one, and we made him memorize his address for future reference.

Chuck Fontenot, Assistant Chief
Clearwater Fire Department
Clearwater, Louisiana

The Party Hat

*We are all here for a spell, get all the good
laughs you can.*

Will Rogers

It was a beautiful Southern California day with the
sun shining through the open windows of the
Captain's perfectly arranged office. April 13, 1975 was
my first day as a firefighter with the Costa Mesa Fire
Department. The birds chirped outside with such
fanfare that it was hard, especially for this nervous
and intimidated rookie, to concentrate on what my
Captain was saying, but I was.

"Your position on the fire truck is directly behind
me," he boomed. "On medical calls you are to bring the
medical box and will be responsible for asking the
appropriate questions and treating the patient." I was

the only one on the crew who was an EMT (Emergency Medical Technician).

"On fires you are to stay at my side and do what I tell you to do, nothing more, nothing less ... period!" he bellowed sternly.

He began to tell me what my duties were around the station when a loud bell rang causing me to jump in my seat. By the time I realized it was my first call, Captain Locke was out the door and standing by the electro-writer waiting for the address. I could hear our dispatcher over the loudspeaker say something about a kid with his head stuck, but was unable to make out the rest.

I quickly took my place on the fire truck and realized that I was about to have my first real-life emergency situation. This wasn't the classroom. This was for real! The only thing I remember about the ride was the sound of the siren and Captain Locke's booming voice over the siren giving directions to the Engineer. My mind was a scrambled mosaic of endless possibilities and solutions, while my stomach was tied in knots. The sound of the air brakes being set and Captain Locke saying, "Let's go!" woke me from my stupor.

I immediately rushed to the rear of the fire engine and retrieved the medical box from its compartment. I stood dutifully at my Captain's side with the medical box in hand, when he knocked on the front door of the house. A four-year-old boy answered the door with what appeared to be a party hat on his head and a big smile.

I immediately thought, "What a beautiful Saturday morning for a birthday party."

The little boy greeted us. "Hello sir, you must be here for me," he said proudly.

The mother hurried over to the door and, while opening the screen door to let us in, explained her predicament. As the screen door opened I could see that this was not a party hat, but a metal sand pail sitting on this boy's head, with the handle of the pail wrapping underneath his chin as a chin strap on a hat would do. She had tried unsuccessfully to take the pail off of her son's head and was meeting her mother-in-law for lunch. She couldn't possibly take her son to a restaurant with a sand pail stuck on his head ... could we please help her.

My Captain immediately turned to me and said, "Yoder, go get me the pry bar."

Well, this is a four-foot-long metal bar with a narrow blade on one end used to pry open car doors, front doors to homes, and anything else you want to destroy. With the pride of knowing exactly where to find this tool, and the confidence of knowing how to use it, I took off for the fire engine. In less than thirty seconds I returned with pry bar in hand, ready to go to work, only to find that my Captain had removed the pail from the boy's head by using nothing more than his bare hands and a little ingenuity. Captain Locke, looking up at me, gave me a wink and it was then that I realized he was only kidding about the pry bar. I suddenly felt quite humbled and very ridiculous standing there with this large tool of destruction.

And, so, my *real life* experiences had begun as a firefighter—thanks to an adventurous little boy and a well-seasoned Fire Captain.

Curt Yoder, Firefighter
Costa Mesa Fire Department
Costa Mesa, California

Rookies

The Heart of the Fire Service ...
There's a 'Rookie' in All of Us

The Rookie

In youth we learn; in age we understand.
Marie Von Ebner-Eschenbach

A gray haze filled the bunkroom of the firehouse this morning. No, it wasn't smoke or the unkempt evidence of married men, who for the last twenty-four hours reverted back to bachelorhood. This haze was the sun's haunting pre-dawn hue that seems to sneak through the blinds every morning.

I rolled over just enough to be chilled by the cold breeze of the fan. The fan, of course, was used to cover up the snoring of a few good firefighters that all too often denied even the remotest possibility of any glottal eruptions on their part. The coldness was interrupted, if only for a few moments, by the welcome smell of fresh coffee brewing in the kitchen.

I could see through the sullen haze that the rookie of the station was already up and going about his chores, as he was every morning.

Since my promotion, I can't remember the last time I emptied the dishwasher or ran the vacuum over the dayroom floor. I sometimes see Mel Brooks' face and hear his comical retort, "It's good to be king." Not that I feel above the work, but the rookie is so dedicated to doing his part, and then some. He seems to have really bought into the idea of duty and pride, as we all did, in his eagerness to embrace the sometimes distasteful blend of duty and tradition. I often ask myself if I were ever that dutiful. As a matter of fact, I sometimes envy that eagerness and undaunted energy that he and so many other young rookies display day after day.

My energy has never fizzled out; nor has my desire to do this job. I still revel in the thought of easing someone's pain. I find great satisfaction in mitigating an otherwise chaotic situation; yes, I even find an unexplainable pleasure in vacuuming the floor. No veteran ever loses his or her desire to do this job. We all continue for one great reason—tradition. And who, but a rookie, could instill that continued sense of pride in a fifteen- or twenty-year veteran?

Pour me a cup of that JOE rookie! Sit down over here and let me tell you what this job is all about. If you don't mind, I'd like to just sit here and listen to you dream about your future expectations of glory and honor in this service, this fire service; for it is you rookie that keeps my own thoughts of past glory and honor alive. It's you rookie that allows me to find the second wind when I think I'm too tired. It's you again that allows this humanity to continue in our community. Someday you'll be in my shoes. Of course, I'll be retired and gone fish'n ... but you'll be right here drinking JOE and dreaming ... with a rookie. Don't let the other guys know I told you this rookie, but I appreciate what you do.

The shift was over and the rookie stashed away his gear so it wouldn't be maliciously yet playfully frozen in the kitchen freezer. He looked at his captain and they both just smiled in quiet simultaneous affirmation.

He walked to the parking lot just as the alarm tones broke the morning's quiet. He turned in time to see Engine and Rescue Company 11 respond to a fire alarm. As the truck went by, the rookie's captain leaned out the window and shouted, "My God, I love this job." *Me too,* said the rookie quietly to himself. *Me too.*

Barry "Skip" Wilson, Captain
Littleton Fire Department
Littleton, Colorado

The Apron

Humor is just another defense against the universe.

Mel Brooks

A rookie firefighter had a well-earned reputation as a *know it all.* One day his Lieutenant told him to hose off the apron. An *apron* is the Fire Service vernacular for the concrete that sits in front of the apparatus doors.

About an hour later the Lieutenant checked on the apron. It was still bone dry. He asked the other firefighters if they had seen the rookie firefighter, and was told he was in the kitchen.

Approaching the rookie, the Lieutenant said, "I asked you to hose off the apron an hour ago and it is still bone dry."

The rookie hesitantly replied, "I've been looking for an apron in this kitchen for over an hour and can't find one."

Marc D. Greenwood, Lieutenant
Akron Fire Department
Akron, Ohio

Jokes 'R' Us

... A time to laugh.
Ecclesiastes 3A: 1 and 4B

If a person wanted to write a manual on practical jokes, the average fire station should not be overlooked. Firefighters frequently have idle time on their hands, and what better way to spend this time than finding clever ways to get the best of a new comrade.

The primary target is the rookie, and a new guy's first day means nothing less than a barrage of practical jokes. My first shift was no different.

On that memorable first day, I found guys jumping out of the large trash dumpster when I was chosen to take the garbage out at ten o'clock at night, and that was just the beginning. Clean-up duties completed, I jumped in the shower and soaped up just as the tones went off. I wasn't about to miss a call on this, my first shift, so I jumped out, still half covered with soap, threw on my jumpsuit, ran to the pole and, because I was wet, didn't exactly slide down with a controlled grip. Instead I literally flew down the pole trying desperately, but awkwardly, to slow my descent. I hit the bottom padding on the truck room floor. Loud laughter accompanied my bump. "False alarm, Tommy."

I laughed and secretly hoped this was the end of the pranks.

Wrong!

We went back upstairs and things chilled out a bit. Then, one of them told me about a dish that didn't get washed and would I kindly take care of it before going to bed. (Yes, rookies get dish duty, too.) They acted so serious and matter-of-fact that I really thought I had missed a dish. Besides, I reasoned that the jokes had now ended. Well, I went to the sink, hit the lever to turn the water on, and instinctively jumped back as I was hit with a hard stream of water from the side sprayer. They had rubber-banded it wide open. Another laugh on the new guy's initiation day.

Things finally settled down, and one by one the guys went back into the dorm to go to bed. Within a few minutes I was the only one left in the day room. Again, I gullibly reasoned that these guys had had

their fun and now they were going to bed. Not wanting
to be the oddball, I figured I'd do the same. I grabbed
my boots, walked back, and gently opened the dorm
room door. I stepped inside. The dorm was deathly
quiet and pitch black. *Man, these guys don't fool
around when it's sack time*, I thought. I knew I dared
not turn on any lights, so I waited for my eyes to
adjust before moving. All I needed to do was stumble
over someone's bed, land on him in it, and destroy the
rest of my career!

After a few seconds I slowly crept toward the
general direction of my bed. The room was big and it
accommodated twelve bunks. The last thing I wanted
to do was blindly tap the wrong one, which would be
another career-ruining move! But I felt confident as I
neared what I knew was my bed. I brushed my leg up
against the foot end and could tell by the material I
had made it. *Home free*, I thought.

Still unable to see, I guided myself around the side
of my bed and leaned over to quietly place my boots on
the floor. But before I stood up, a scary animal roar
rang out behind me as I was pushed onto my bunk.
Not only was I startled to death, but I landed on a hard
human-like figure buried underneath my cover, which
scared me even more. I jumped off to the sounds of
massive laughter in the room.

I hit the bed light and pulled off the covers to unveil the rescue mannequin. "Lord, let this be all," I prayed boldly out loud.

Finally, I fell asleep. The rest of the night was call free, and more importantly, practical joke free except, of course, for the gentle coating of flour under the covers that added one more round of laughter in the morning before shift change.

Tommy Neiman, Firefighter/Paramedic
Fort Pierce/Saint Lucie County Fire District
Fort Pierce, Florida
As told in Sirens for the Cross by Tommy Neiman with
Sue Reynolds

I'm Going to Make it ... After All

*I know of no more encouraging fact than the
unquestionable ability of man to elevate his life
by a conscious endeavor.*

Henry David Thoreau

When I applied to my hometown Alexandria-St.
Albans Township Fire Department in 1990, it
was a small volunteer organization with as many
livestock as residents. Squad runs were limited, and
fire runs were scarcer. To become a member of this fire
department, a six month probationary period was
required, at which time you were voted on by the
Firefighter's Association. I was told from the first day
that you were accepted as a member *only* if the other
firefighters and squad personnel liked you *and* you put
forth some extra effort.

I came on in the summer and waited to begin
classes to become an Emergency Medical Technician

and Firefighter. It was common practice to send probationary members through the necessary education prior to their acceptance because there was always a need for additional help in an emergency. I was one of a handful of women in this department. Most of the women had no interest in fighting fires, and the few who took the classes generally did not have, nor want, an active role in firefighting. I was not going to allow myself to be labeled passive or unambitious.

I entered the probationary rite of passage, and my hand became molded to the push broom. I could sweep and hose down the bay floors without breaking a sweat. Need a pack horse? I'd carry whatever anyone needed to prove I was a worthy investment, not lacking the physical strength of my male probationary counterparts. But, alas, my forte was cleaning the medic unit and engine. I would wash and wax them on any opportunity I had, much to the delight of the old timers who always found a spot or two that I missed.

Our fire department hosts an annual fundraising carnival that has become the community's homecoming. There are rides, tractor pulls, and the beloved parade on the last day of the carnival. As a tradition, the fire department takes every piece of apparatus through the parade. We had two engines, two squads, and a grass truck.

I knew that unless I was there early, I would be
forced to endure the parade in the back of the medic. I
arrived at the firehouse three hours prior to the start
of the parade. I cleaned the exterior of the first-out
squad and engine, making sure that every piece of
chrome shined and that the windows would sparkle in
the sun. I got out the automotive protectant, used for
shining and protecting vinyl, leather and rubber, and
laboriously cleaned each tire. Soon, it was time to
tackle the interior cab of the engine. It seemed that no
one had ever taken the time to thoroughly clean the
bench seat or dash. This, I decided, would be my vote
clincher for membership, as well as a coveted seat on
the engine for the parade. Like a mad woman, I
scrubbed the seats with soap and water. Somehow, it
still lacked that parade shine. The vinyl protectant was
the only solution. I meticulously shined every part of
the interior visible to the naked eye. The seats shone
like they were brand new. I was so sure that I'd
stumbled upon an untapped source of votes, that I
decided to shine the seats of the squad too.

It was parade time, and I sat down in the center of
the bench seat on the first-out engine. I had told no
one of the good deed I had done—I wanted them to
notice it themselves so I wouldn't seem so desperate
for their votes. As I've learned, it is typically a frenzy at

the start of our parade. The driver and the officer took their seats on either side of me, candy in hand for the kids along the parade route. Finally, we were on our way.

No one seemed to notice the glistening seats until the engine had to brake suddenly when the parade came to a grinding halt. The driver was seat belted, but the officer and I met the dash and windshield head on! No one was hurt but the officer and I were both stunned. We were going slowly, and I didn't under-stand what had happened.

The officer didn't say a word until we got back to the firehouse. There he informed me why the seats were never shined with vinyl protectant. It made the seats slippery. He wanted to know the last time that the fire engine responded on a run at 15 mph, on a road with no curves, cars or sudden stops. The subse-quent ribbing and jokes were quite entertaining for the rest of the crew, who took delight in learning about the *slippery seat incident*.

I was banned from the vinyl protectant, but not from the fire department. It seems the Firefighters Association members found the entire matter quite humorous, and voted me on, if for nothing more than comic relief.

I have since made it my mission on the fire department to not only fight fire, protect property and save lives, but to educate the innocent new probies on the *perils* of using vinyl protectant on our engine seats.

Johneen "Jay" Castle, Firefighter/EMT
Alexandria-St. Albans Township Fire Department
Alexandria, Ohio

A Tribute to Our Fallen

We stand at attention as you pass us ...
One final time ...

Firefighter, Teacher, Friend

*Dedicated by Michael R. Chase, in memory of
fellow firefighter Captain David Watts of the
Nantucket Fire Department, who suffered a
heart attack in the line of duty on May 2, 1999.*

We stand at attention as you pass us, one final time.

Each of us stands silently at parade rest, hands clasped in front, shoulders relaxed. The Marshal's cry brings us to full attention as he calls for salute. The honor guard hoists its colors as the pallbearers carry out their somber duty.

I look from face to face, friend to friend, and read the emotions, the stories. The wail of bagpipes breaks the silence, mournful and enlightening all in the same note. I close my eyes and I am immediately awash with a lifetime of memories.

Your wave every day, passing on the road.

Arriving on a scene to find you, solid and professional yet flushed with excitement as if each was your first call.

Surrounded by flame in a burning building, your hand on my back, lending nerve to this new firefighter. A sure grip on the steering wheel of the rescue as we work to calm a frightened child. Hauling equipment to a second story roof, knowing I need not be concerned with the ascent when I look down to see you footing my ladder.

Learning from your slow, measured steps as you approach an accident scene, identifying the hazards before they become so. Knowing you from the other sweaty, soot covered forms hunched on the engine's back step after a call, your soft voice and quiet laughter so individual to you.

The bagpipes fade to silence and I open my eyes. We fall in and prepare to begin our final march. We lay you to rest, the first and last rest you'll know as a firefighter. Your diligence allowed you none, your dedication knew no peace.

You died as we all wish to, in the line of duty. You passed upholding the oath we have all sworn.

I look around and see little sorrow from the many professionals standing stiffly at attention in your honor. I see gratitude for the privilege of having known you. I see pride for the devotion with which you served the needs of your community so selflessly. I see regret with the loss of a brother, from such a close family.

We stand at attention as you pass us, one final time ... and say goodbye.

Michael R. Chase, Firefighter/EMT
Nantucket Fire Department
Nantucket, Massachusetts

A Silent Alarm

A Silent Alarm is heard and heartfelt
by firefighters' wives around the world.

Patricia Rannigan

An Angel was watching

And took my loved one away.

From time and from sin

This Angel took my loved one in.

And this Angel draped him

With angel wings;

My loved one fluttered

Into open heavens.

When I hear

My Angel with wings,

Begin to sing,

    I will feel my Fireman smile.

I will know I'll be with

    My Love again—

        And the joy of happiness

            I remember him giving me here.

I will experience,

    Once again,

        All of this sealed in my

            Burning heart,

As I give my

    final

        farewell ...

Patricia Rannigan. Wife of Firefighter David Rannigan
Norfolk Fire and Paramedical Services
Chesapeake, Virginia

No Greater Love
A Letter to My Fallen Brother

Greater love has no one than this, than to
lay down one's life for his friends.

John 15:13

You were my best friend, my brother, my brother in
battle, and my daughter's Godfather.

So many hats to wear and so little time to wear
them. You gave your life unselfishly, so that many
others might live.

Every time I climb into my turn-outs I have to stop
and say a little prayer for you and ask that you watch
over me as I do the job we both love so very much. I
miss you more than I can tell you and no one will ever
be able to fill that space in my heart that you hold.

I learned so much from you, yet there are many
chapters now that I have to write without you. I don't
go a day without thinking of you and all the good times

that we shared. I do know that one day we shall see each other again, but until that day my friend ... I have a HUGE hole in my life that you once filled.

I will always remember what you said to me the night you left us, I will cherish it forever. "Greater love has no one than this, than to lay down one's life for his friends." John 15:13.

Robert W. Tennies, Volunteer Firefighter,
Hydrant Hose Company 1
City of Geneva Fire Department, New York
Career Federal Firefighter
NAS Oceana, Fort Drum, New York

Editors Note:

This letter was written in loving memory of Timothy J. Warren III, who died in the line of duty on February 15, 1997. Timothy's only brother, Ronald F. Warren, also was killed in the line of duty, on May 16, 1980. Both brothers were members of Hydrant Hose Company No. 1, Geneva Fire Department in Geneva, New York. Their father, Timothy Warren, Jr. also served as a member of the Geneva Fire Department for 52 years before he died of congestive heart failure in January, 2000.

Timmy's and Ron's mother, Marilyn, is an active volunteer with the National Fallen Firefighters

Foundation. She continually reaches out to other families who have lost beloved firefighters in the line of duty, easing their pain through shared memories.

You Only Know Him Now

Choose to think of him as a hero in death and I will tell you that he was a hero in life.

Jon McDuffie

We provide a faceless, nameless service to a community that rarely knows how much they need us. We are a myriad of thousands, each with our own personalities, families and troubles. A band of anonymous heroes that subordinates ego and self-interest to serve a populace that only knows that we will be there when they call. We get paid for what we are able to do, on the occasions when we are called to do it.

This week, one of us got a name, a face, a rank, a family ... a life beyond a badge. His life is now recognized, only because it was sacrificed. He gave his life defending the property of a person he did not know, in a City that did not know him.

His name is Joseph Dupee.

I knew him before you and will remember him long after his name wanes in your short-term memory.

Ten mornings a month, Joe rose before the sun, kissed his sleeping family goodbye, and made the drive to his second home. He exercised, he trained himself and his crew, he laughed, he sulked, and he handled tedious projects. He read his Bible and spoke about it with others. He shared his opinions at the kitchen table with his brothers and sisters who drank thousands of cups of bad coffee with him, all the while attempting to solve the problems of the world. And then he would wait—for the calls where he sometimes worked harder than you can imagine.

Some of his work days were spent waiting. Some days his City did not need him as much as other days, but still, he waited. If you needed Joe for small things—a broken water pipe, a child locked in a car, a pot of beans that cooked just a bit too long—he responded to your call. Other times, when you needed him for life threatening emergencies—to rescue you from natural and man made disasters, from fire, from accidents, from illness, from yourselves—he responded to your call. You never doubted that Joe would be there for you. You never knew his name and he never asked you to justify your need. He served you because he wanted to help, and he loved to help you. You could have stopped giving him pay raises, repairing his station, hiring more firefighters, and he would still be waiting to answer your call.

Joe loved his family, his God, and his country. He was an opinionated prankster who loved to talk, could not cook, and drove too fast behind the wheel of a fire engine. He was a good fire ground officer who worked aggressively at incidents and diligently at his post. He was on my platoon for three years—he will be my brother always. But you did not know him then. You only know him now.

Choose to think of him as a hero in death and I will tell you that he was a hero in life. Use Joe's memory for sadness, and I will use it to comfort his family and my brothers and sisters that must continue to wait. Continue pouring out sympathy until it becomes a faint trickle and I will still be here waiting for the next call.

I provide a faceless, nameless service to a community that rarely knows how much they need me. If I am called from a sound sleep to sacrifice my life attempting to save the life or property of someone I do not know, I will do so without regret.

Joe did it. Why wouldn't I?

The Heart Behind the Hero

Jon McDuffie, Firefighter
Los Angeles City Fire Department
Los Angeles, California

Written in loving memory of Joseph Charles Dupee, who died in the line of duty on March 8, 1998, while serving with the Los Angeles City Fire Department.

Roll of Honor

Our Fallen Brothers & Sisters

As recognized by the

National Fallen Firefighters Foundation

At the

National Fallen Firefighters Memorial

Emmitsburg, Maryland

1981-1999

To live in hearts we leave behind

is not to die.

Author Unknown

Roll of Honor

Alabama Fallen Firefighters

1981 Sherry K. Garner
1983 James D. Overstreet
1984 Gerard DeJohn
1986 Randy E. Patrick
1987 David A. Damron
1987 Virginia Faye Bolton
1988 Tommy W. Hale
1989 Warren Allen Williford, Jr.
1989 James Edward Johnson
1989 Milton W. Keammerar
1989 J. B. Rose
1990 Carrol D. Marvel
1990 James Earl Ray
1991 John R. Cochran
1992 James J. Cothran
1992 James A. Bennett
1994 Herbert T. Smith
1994 Joseph Jay Boothe
1994 Bedford V. Cash
1995 Lathan G. Smith, Jr.
1995 Travis McCormick
1996 William R. Reid
1996 Martha A. Bice
1997 Tommy T. Gross, III
1997 Ricky Gene Moore
1998 Tulon Lee Goodwin
1998 Johnnie Ray Park
1999 Roger McEwen, Sr.

Alaska Fallen Firefighters

1991 Christine A. Pennington

Arizona Fallen Firefighters

1981 Ronald J. McNeeley, Jr.

1983 Herman Peyton
1984 Ricky S. Pearce
1986 Jack R.Stevens
1987 Samuel M. McAnally
1987 Richard Y. Garza
1989 Ronald J. Cannon
1989 James Martz
1990 Joseph L.Chacon
1990 Sandra J. Bachman
1990 Alex S. Contreras
1990 James L. Denney
1990 Curtis E. Springfield
1990 James E. Ellis
1991 L. Wayne Struble
1991 Robert F. Million
1992 Calvin Morris
1994 Ronald E. Holmgreen
1994 Timothy J. Hale
1996 Michelle Smith
1997 Jesse D. Gates
1997 Leo A. Stevens
1998 Jerry D. Donahue

Arkansas Fallen Firefighters

1981 Lloyd Whiteside
1984 James H. Frizzell
1984 Edwin G. Murphy
1984 Thurman P. Keener, Jr.
1985 Ronald C. Edgmon
1986 Glen Edward Miller
1986 Jeffrey D. Copeland
1987 Allie Odell Egger
1989 Louis Caracciolo
1989 Raymond A. Frampton
1992 George Delbert Weischman
1992 Billy Ray Powell
1994 James Newt Morgan

Roll of Honor

Arkansas Fallen Firefighters

1995 Dania Stivers
1995 Randy Williford
1996 Robert Pemberton
1997 Stewart Warren
1997 Reginald G. Robinson
1997 Edward Lee "Bo" Hudson
1998 Ernest Alan McElroy
1999 Wade Meshell
1999 Jerry W. Ramey
1999 Martin R. Wauson

California Fallen Firefighters

1981 Gilbert Lopez
1981 Donald E. Moore
1981 William J. Anger
1981 Dean W. Rhoades
1981 Thomas G. Taylor
1981 Robert E. Sparks
1982 Gerald N. Vosburgh
1982 James H. Raines
1982 Scott A. Karnitz
1982 James P. Eakin
1983 Henry D. Salas
1983 Jerry V. Litell
1983 Michel S. Chenard
1983 Clifton A. Graves
1983 John A. Yoder
1983 Gilbert G. Hund
1983 Jerald J. Hisel
1984 Benjamin Pinel
1984 Michael P. Mattioda
1984 Earl L. Hilliard
1984 David Gardella
1984 Jose A. Silva
1984 Raymond E. Eichert

1985 W. Phillip Saaranzin
1985 Guy F. Baquet
1985 Alvin M. Brown
1985 Robert W. Jahelka
1985 Ron Hubbard
1986 Ronald Dean Marsh
1986 Dennis J. Donelson
1987 William M. Berg
1987 Denis Lee Cullins
1987 William P. Schmidt, Jr.
1987 Sir Isaac Lindsay, Jr.
1987 David R. Erickson
1987 Donald H. Gormley
1987 Stephen P. Harrell
1987 Gary M. Hischier
1987 Donn Johnson
1987 William G. Davis
1987 Charles W. Peterson
1987 Bruce F. Visser
1987 Freddie Pahnemah
1988 Charles V. Watkins
1988 Charles R. Sager
1988 David Daniel
1988 Gail Gene Nobel
1989 Bill M. Mehaffey
1989 Robert M. Chollman
1989 Peter D. Rose
1989 James F. Starnes
1989 Antonio S. Hernandez
1990 Kenneth E. Enslow
1990 Bennie B. Collins
1990 Clayton M. Cutter
1990 Vidar D. Anderson
1990 Mark Allan Moore
1990 Aaron J. Perry
1990 Lance J. Petersen
1990 Victor Ferrera
1991 Marshal E. Viloria
1991 John Robert Sieglinger

Roll of Honor

California Fallen Firefighters

1991 Robert Allen Shaw
1991 James M. Riley, Jr.
1991 Wayne L. Pulley
1991 Donald V. Mello
1991 Gifford Keeth
1991 James E. Howe
1991 Lou Falconer
1992 Leonard D. Martin
1992 Roger E. Stark
1992 Roc E. Manchester
1992 Charles Frost Sheridan
1993 Steve H. Brown
1993 Rick A. Vreeland
1993 Christopher C. Rutledge
1993 Arthur Ruezga
1993 Randy W. Reynaga
1993 Tony F. Mendonsa, Jr.
1993 Jeffrey M. Langley
1993 Jerry E. Butler
1993 Christopher D. Herman
1994 David Castro
1994 Roger A. Evans
1994 Joseph W. Johnson
1994 Shawn D. Zaremba
1994 Robert L. Buc
1995 Lisa Netsch
1995 Wendell W. Ayers
1995 Gary Cockrell
1995 Ray H. Lencioni
1995 Raymond Trygar
1995 Michael A. Lohbeck
1995 Michael Smith
1995 Louis Mambretti
1995 Judith L. Luster-Stauss
1996 Jack Lee Hone
1997 David Michael Ray
1997 Joseph James Estavillo

1997 Bryan Jacob Golden
1997 Floyd Dean Hiser, Sr.
1997 Kenneth E. Bayer
1997 Brett A. Laws
1997 Michael A. Gilberg
1997 David Robert Kyle
1998 Michael A. Butler
1998 Brian Keith Carrasco
1998 Joseph Charles Dupee
1998 Michael D. McComb
1998 Gary D. Nagel
1998 Michael A. Pizinger
1998 Eric F. Reiner
1998 Thomas Oscar Wall
1998 Duane Williams
1999 Matthew E. Black
1999 Stephen J. Masto
1999 Clifford T. "Tom" Moore
1999 Karen J. Savage
1999 Martin Stiles
1999 Tracy Dolan Toomey

Colorado Fallen Firefighters

1981 John M. Wood
1982 William J. Duran, Sr.
1982 Scott L. Smith
1982 Richard D. Watts
1983 George R. Burton
1984 Colin P. Boast
1985 Richard A. McConnell
1986 Lee S. Steingoetter
1986 Darrel D. Sutton
1986 Harold Siewers
1986 Phillip T. Hamilton
1987 August J. Valentine
1988 Scott Allen Reynolds
1988 James L. Seela
1988 Barry H. Halvorsen

Roll of Honor

Colorado Fallen Firefighters

1989 John Patrick Hager
1991 Kevin D. Keel
1992 Mark W. Langvardt
1992 Richard E. Wilson
1993 Douglas K. Konecny
1994 Richard K. Tyler
1995 Martin G. Kautz
1998 Charles Franklin Key

Connecticut Fallen Firefighters

1981 Allan J. Turner
1981 Francis G. Casale
1981 Thomas J. Garrahy
1981 Richard F. Kelleher
1981 William J. Kenny
1981 Ernest B. Osborne
1981 Frederick H. Letsch, Jr.
1982 Francis D. Federici, Sr.
1982 Joseph L. Halas
1982 Martin R. Melody
1982 Henry J. Savage
1982 Thomas E. Lovett, Sr.
1983 Arleigh M. Christensen
1983 Albert F. McGovern, Sr.
1983 Arthur E. Mattson, Jr.
1984 Roger F. Sullivan
1984 Francis E. Burns
1984 Leonard S. Guerrera
1984 Anthony L. Conforte
1985 Russell H. Jones
1986 Richard L. Tomlinson
1986 George A. Kelly
1986 William M. Hathaway
1986 Joseph A. Daddona
1987 Richard N. Vallillo

1987 A. Arthur Vincent
1987 George R. Charak
1987 John A. Bertolini
1989 Russell W. Musante, Sr.
1990 Gary M. Passaro
1990 Heriberto T. Rivera
1990 Howard A. Hughes
1991 Daniel E. Wannagot
1991 Michael Moriarty
1991 Robert Allison Cole
1991 Ronald C. Altieri
1992 Robert S. Heide, Sr.
1992 Joseph Kirchner
1993 John M. O'Connor
1993 George Blanusa
1994 Mark L. Mitchell
1995 Edward Pitcher
1996 Edward Francis Ramos
1996 Craig Michael Arnone
1999 Walter J. Flyntz

Delaware Fallen Firefighters

1982 H. Thomas Tucker
1990 James Goode, Jr.
1997 W. Jack Northam
1998 Prince A. Mousley, Jr.

District of Columbia Fallen Firefighters

1983 Calvin L. Steve
1984 John T. Williams
1987 Clifford R. Oliver
1997 John Michael Carter
1999 Louis J. Matthews
1999 Anthony Sean "Sauce" Phillips, Sr.
1999 Costello N. Robinson

Roll of Honor

Florida Fallen Firefighters

1981 Franz G. Warner
1981 Stewart T. Baker
1981 Gary N. Turner
1981 William Ziegler
1981 Robert C. Lamme
1981 Scott J. Maness
1981 Issac Royal, Jr.
1981 William C. Runyon
1981 Beau W. Sauselein
1983 David B. Manetzke
1983 Donald C. Lund
1983 Eddie F. Jackson
1983 Robert L. Baltimore
1983 Athniel K. Appelberg
1983 Ellis A. Williams, Jr.
1984 Michael T. McCarthy
1984 Jack L. Pratt, Sr.
1985 Randall O. Garrett
1985 Frank R. Vigh
1985 Robert D. Tabor
1985 Marco A. Miranda
1985 Shawn T. O'Dare
1986 William E. Albritton
1986 Edgar A. Cowart
1986 George R. Kennedy
1986 Timothy J. Wells
1987 James A. Parks
1987 Peter A. Codella
1987 Karl J. Carman, Jr.
1987 Loran L. Cochran
1988 Robert J. Padgett
1988 Jeffery W. Holt
1988 Joseph R. Barrett
1989 Ervin W. Fort
1989 Paul J. Reid
1989 Todd Aldridge
1989 Mark A. Benge

1990 James C. Winters
1990 Karl J. Drews
1990 Kaye F. Anderson
1990 Leon Lamar Benton
1990 Rufus J. Harrison
1991 James D. Sapp
1991 Mark A. Wilkes
1992 Frank Albert Smith
1992 John M. Byers, Jr.
1993 Louis Todd Powers
1993 Larry Russell Harris, Jr.
1993 Keith A. Walker
1993 Everett C. Pierce
1994 Ann F. Sheppard
1994 Ronald W. Russell
1994 Dewey F. Henry
1995 Lyle Garlinghouse
1997 Malcolm A. Rovero, II
1997 David Shawn Williams
1998 Richard "Keith" Rice, Sr.
1999 David T. Nall

Georgia Fallen Firefighters

1981 Earl Taft
1981 Scott D. Duncan
1981 George F. Hilton
1981 Benjamin B. Watkins, Jr.
1981 James D. Cox
1982 Joseph G. Bostwick
1982 Raymond L. Waters
1982 James H. Carter
1983 Jackie R. Gober
1984 Dennis C. Martin
1984 William A. Satterfield
1985 Michael A. Gurley
1985 William M. Freeman, Jr.
1985 James E. Smith
1985 Bobby Lee Carter

Roll of Honor

Georgia Fallen Firefighters

1986 Gary Carter Pruitt
1986 Jerry A. Prince
1986 John Curtis Barker
1987 Michael T. Foster
1987 Larry C. Kent
1987 Charles W. Duren
1988 Barney Russell Riner
1988 Richard F. Mullis
1990 Curtis C. Thomason
1990 Steve L. Girardot
1990 John W. Folds
1991 Normal Lewis Simmons
1991 Alfornia Hollis
1994 Mary Jo Brown
1995 Bobby Crowe
1995 Lisa Batten
1996 Charles Brantley Chesney
1996 Robert Hamler
1996 Marcel S. Glenn
1996 George Russell Crane, Jr.
1997 Will Ellis Rowe, Jr.
1997 Richard Cullen Jenkins
1998 Kennon Loy Williams
1999 Lewis Edward Williams

Hawaii Fallen Firefighters

1984 Henry Y.S. Sur
1992 Darrell R. Nam
1995 Peter Alan Crown
1996 Mark P. Clark
1996 Steven Gushiken

Idaho Fallen Firefighters

1984 Dale J. Uptmor

1986 Gerald J. Franz
1986 Anthony M. Pecos
1986 Cordell W. Stewart
1986 Andrew V. Waquie
1986 Benjamin P. Waquie
1986 Allen M. Baca
1988 Kevin A. Monroe
1988 Posey Phillips
1991 William F. Martin
1992 Clifford L. Herman
1992 Julie Ann Young
1994 Robert L. Johnson
1994 Roger W. Roth
1994 Daren James Smith
1994 James R. Thrash
1995 Bill Buttram
1995 Josh Oliver

Illinois Fallen Firefighters

1981 Walter F. Mcgraw
1981 Jerome F. Srejma
1981 Thomas C. Harry
1981 Terry K. Berg
1981 Myron A. Alford
1981 Dean L. Rawson
1981 Joseph R. Hitz
1981 William C. Lasley
1981 Thomas M. Lydon
1981 Samuel L. Taylor
1981 Gary M. Michalek
1981 Craig McShane
1982 Orville J. Soens
1982 Thomas M. Pierce
1982 Michael D. Taylor
1982 Robert W. Danaher
1983 Kenneth J. Sobbe
1983 John H. Marnati
1983 Nieves Luna, Sr.

Roll of Honor

Illinois Fallen Firefighters

1983 Vernon A. Gudat
1983 Hubert W. Golden
1983 David O. Erickson
1983 Wayne M. Turpin
1983 Huey Copeland
1983 Lawrence J. Bleichner
1983 Sidney Brown
1983 Joseph F. Shipton
1984 Belle C. Sullivan-Weiss
1984 Barney O. Staggs
1984 Charles R. Staggs
1984 Dale A. Whitmarsh
1984 James J. Lausch
1984 Christopher I. Watkins
1984 Thomas Baron
1984 David E. Foecking
1984 Katherine A. Hughes
1984 Perry E. Parker
1984 Robert F. Pleski
1984 Lothar C. Cogar
1984 Kenneth E. Armour
1984 Philip Kenneally
1985 Michael A. Talley, Sr.
1985 Mariano F. Leoni
1985 Michael L. Forchione
1985 Rayond J. Magnus
1985 Daniel A. Nockels
1985 Camella D. Kohl
1985 Bernard O. Rogers
1985 Franklin W. Mercer
1985 James K. Allen
1985 Raymond M. Sidwell
1986 Teddy Jezuit
1986 Robert J. Liesz
1986 John Hurter
1986 Edmond P. Coglianese
1987 James E. Hill

1987 Donald Wilson
1987 Russell Allen Winchester
1987 Charles Clark
1987 Richard P. O'Connor
1988 Wilburn R. Ellis
1988 Dana A. Schoolman
1989 Kelvin L. Anderson
1989 Douglas P. Maicach
1989 John B. Meisch
1989 Frank A. Cornell
1989 Joseph L. Samec
1990 Robert J. Ely
1990 Ken M. Herington
1990 Thomas H. Maxeiner
1991 John H. Spencer
1991 Mark S. Rice
1991 George S. Winckler
1992 Robert Medlicott
1992 Gary S. Porter
1992 Richard C. Heller, Jr.
1992 Tim L. Lewis
1992 Patrick J. Luby
1992 Eldon W. Harrison
1992 Kim Meredith
1993 Steven J. McNamee
1993 Edwin R. Conklin
1993 Delmar M. Mondy
1993 Dennis R. Olson
1995 John J. Haviar
1995 Donald J. Kaczka
1995 Thomas O'Boyle
1996 Stanley E. Scott
1996 Kevin Woodrow Reveal
1996 Robert L. Duvall
1996 Dale Richard Zimmerman
1996 Martin Doherty
1997 Lawrence Hobson
1997 Brian Thomas Hauk
1997 Walter Douglas Buckert

Roll of Honor

Illinois Fallen Firefighters

1997 Michael F. Drobitsch
1997 Howard E. Strube, Jr.
1997 Michael Dean Mapes
1997 Jesse F. Stewart
1998 Eugene W. Blackmon, Jr.
1998 William Bonnar, Sr.
1998 Patrick J. King
1998 Anthony E. Lockhart
1998 Tom E. Prendergast
1999 Ralph J. Loyd
1999 Wayne R. Luecht
1999 Arthur Tullis

Indiana Fallen Firefighters

1981 George R. McCormack
1981 Ricky K. Genth
1981 David L. Vurton
1982 John J. Rossi, Jr.
1982 Brian L. Samuels
1982 James W. Stewart
1982 Alphonse J. Kriscunas
1982 Gary W. Van Vactor
1982 Randall Hansen
1982 Dane R. Hoffhien
1982 Robert B. Kermeen
1984 Roger G. Tharp
1985 Larry D. Filler
1985 Theodore P. Lander
1986 Richard D. Standafer
1986 Jack E. Schafstall
1986 Wilber E. Anderson
1987 William S. Warnock
1987 Robert Earl Hickman
1988 David J. Edwards
1988 William E. Deering, Jr.
1988 Jan P. Dawes

1988 Norman D. Stuart
1989 James C. Pugsley
1990 Richard V. Brekrus
1990 Nicholas W. Hart
1990 Ralph L. Hoppenjans
1991 Fred P. Biedron
1992 Ellwood M. Gelenius
1992 John J. Lorenzano
1994 David H. Barter
1994 James D. Harvey
1994 Roy W. Stephenson
1995 Greg Cussen
1995 John D. Riggins, Jr.
1995 David A. Harness
1995 Herlof T. Hansen III
1995 Ronald Carl Deer
1996 Laura Halsey
1996 Donald Matthew Raibley
1996 John William Swan, II
1997 Jeffrey E. Sammons
1997 Frank D. Gilbert, Jr.
1998 Matthew Paul Casboni
1998 Paul Allen Laux
1998 Jeffrey William Reick
1999 Brian K. Burnett
1999 Jason A. Gouckenour
1999 Terri Hood
1999 Robert Ulrich

Iowa Fallen Firefighters

1981 Walter E. Eberhart
1982 James R. Baker
1982 Michael L. Johnson
1982 Kirk M. Wicker
1984 John D. Evans
1984 Harold L. Hansen
1985 Lyle V. Boone
1985 Wayne H. Burmeister

Roll of Honor

Iowa Fallen Firefighters

1990 William T. Klein
1990 Joseph M. Wilt
1991 John H. Sienknecht
1992 Don L. Milner
1996 Jack L. Grosse
1998 Thomas Archer, Jr.
1998 Larry R. Walsh
1999 Jason L. Bitting
1999 David M. McNally
1999 Nathan R. Tuck

Kansas Fallen Firefighters

1981 Paul D. Glahn
1982 William E. Duncan
1983 Lester D. Shaw
1984 David A. Ball
1985 Jean R. Charles
1985 Leland F. Jones
1986 Richard D. Harbour
1986 Mark Milton Blair
1987 Warren L. Howland
1987 Kevin E. Prichard
1988 C.C. Killingsworth
1988 Marvin D. Wilcox
1989 David A. Scheidegger
1990 Todd David Colton
1991 Raymond Hazuka
1991 Frank L. Butler
1992 Arthur L. Pearson
1992 Wayne E. Walker
1992 Wilbert L. Dyer
1993 Guy E. Post
1995 Gary E. Soupene
1995 Donald Koebel
1996 Norman Adams
1998 Norman Almond

1998 Craig Daniel Brown

Kentucky Fallen Firefighters

1982 Harry W. Jones
1983 Walter T. Hale
1983 William L. Smothers
1983 Smith Carroll
1984 Edgar O. Hardin
1986 Matthew T. Wyatt
1986 Raymond B. Watkins
1986 Robert W. Martin
1987 Kenneth E. Hollon
1987 Basil Vaughn
1987 William M. Schelling
1988 William F. Cox
1988 Earl Watkins
1988 James H. Boggs
1989 Donald Lee Kirkpatrick, II
1990 Barry M. Gray
1990 Ray J. Shenefield
1990 Thomas D. Brashears
1991 John Emerson Spangler
1991 John Randall Adams
1991 Steven E. Bryant
1992 Benny C. Chaney
1993 Gary W. Armstrong
1993 Harold B. Allgood
1993 Raymond Adkins
1993 Cecil Allen Fain
1993 William M. Wheeler
1994 Craig E. Drury
1994 John Strawn Nutter
1995 Richard A. Washburn
1996 Donald Z. Manuel
1997 Charles H. "Chuck" Williams, II
1997 Stoy Lee Geary

Roll of Honor

Kentucky Fallen Firefighters

1998 William Dwight Yankey
1999 Bruce Franklin
1999 Kenneth A. Nickell
1999 Kevin R. Smith

Louisiana Fallen Firefighters

1981 Albert Jenkins
1981 Harvel F. Dulaney
1983 Ernest J. Bergeron
1984 Michael E. Ard
1984 Percy R. Johnson
1984 Alexander K. Polakovich
1985 Charles E. Croy
1986 George E. Anders
1986 Michael R. Veuleman
1987 Michael C. Ginart
1988 Harris J. Doucet, Sr.
1991 Johnny Lewis, Jr.
1991 Wylie J. Morvant
1992 Anthony V. Calhoun
1996 Lawrence "JuJu" Roche
1996 Keith Boudoin
1997 Allen H. Martin, Jr.
1997 George "Andy" Davis
1998 Allen L. Heirtzler
1999 H. Fred Broussard
1999 Paul F. Ezernack, Jr.
1999 Elvis B. Maxwell

Maine Fallen Firefighters

1981 John R. Nichols
1982 Gerard R. Desjardins
1987 Raymond L. Holman, Jr.
1987 Daryl Parker Wells
1987 Herbert Wilder

1987 John P. Theriault
1988 Robert s. Batchelder
1988 Basil L. Curtis
1989 William E. Varney
1989 Ronald B. Codrey
1990 Francis N. McKenzie
1991 Francis E. Nason
1995 Shawn F. O'Brien
1995 Norman Prime
1996 Robert E. Wallinford, Jr.
1998 Donald Martin

Maryland Fallen Firefighters

1981 Francis W. Blackstock
1981 John W. Burch
1981 Thomas J. Levy
1982 David M. Taulton
1983 Michael P. McCarthy
1983 Jeffrey L. Dieter
1984 Henry W. Rayner, Jr.
1984 Walter J. Bawroski, Sr.
1984 James A. Kimbel
1984 Melvin S. Rosewag, Jr.
1985 John T. Killian
1985 Ralph R. Newell
1985 Robert Snyder
1985 Nelson K. Taylor
1986 Merle C. Baker
1986 Edwin E. Raynor
1987 Howard N. Phelps
1987 Winona L. Crum
1988 James P. Weeks
1988 James G. Yvorra
1988 Frederick W. White
1988 Alan P. Sondej
1988 Albert C. Howard
1988 Warren D. Gott
1990 Daniel J. Raskin

Roll of Honor

Maryland Fallen Firefighters

1990 Thomas Weeks
1990 Thomas E. Hicks
1991 John N. Plummer
1991 Robert J. Henry
1991 Clyde A. Burley
1991 Eddie Arthur
1992 James H. Stavely, III
1992 Kenneth M. Hedrick
1992 Herbert B. Campbell
1993 Michael J. Wilcom, Jr.
1993 William M. Overman, Jr.
1994 Alton G. Warren
1995 Earl R. McNeil, Jr.
1995 Robert C. Lapp
1995 Leroy J. Cropper, Jr.
1995 Eric D. Schaefer
1996 Leonardo M. Maguigad, Jr.
1996 Eugene Bauerlien
1996 Sammy Lee Strall
1996 Donald "Steve" Trice, Jr.
1996 William R. Chambers, Jr.
1997 Charles Allen Weber, Sr.
1998 David M. Brinkley
1998 John R. Kennedy
1998 Joseph Kroboth, Jr.
1998 Preston "Pat" Edgar Patterson
1999 Roy K. Crago
1999 Terry L. Myers

Massachusetts Fallen Firefighters

1981 Paul M. Lentini, Jr.
1981 James M. Gibbons
1981 Robert W. Forest
1981 Robert F. Callahan
1981 Robert F. McNeely
1981 James J. Koen
1982 William B. Luce, Jr.
1982 Francis T. Skusevich, Sr.
1982 Russell M. Shea
1982 Raymond V. McSwiggin
1982 Raymond J. Deshaies
1982 Charles J. Czub
1982 Franklin J. Oliver
1983 Edward J. Donovan
1983 Bernard A. Frechette
1983 John L. McDonnell
1983 Warren D. Colby
1983 Michael J. Blanchard, Sr.
1983 Robert J. McPherson
1984 James A. Flanagan
1985 Joseph Lemieux
1985 Richard J. Daley
1985 Roland A. Weatherbee
1985 James D. Ealey
1986 Edward R. Connolly
1986 Louis DeSantis
1986 Thomas L. Conley
1986 John B. Gannon
1986 Herve Y. LeBlanc
1987 Allan A. Wilde
1987 Paul R. Bernard
1988 Paul R. Caron
1988 Anthony Conti, Jr.
1988 Frederick T. Donovan
1989 William F. McGuire, Jr.
1989 Allan W. Whitcomb
1989 Joseph A. Graziano
1990 Hector M. Segura
1990 Roger A. Houghton
1992 Lionel Alves
1993 Jesse Pacheco, Jr.
1993 Richard H. Melloni, Sr.

Roll of Honor

Massachusetts Fallen Firefighters

1993 Francis J. Baker
1993 Peter S. Sadowski
1994 Stephen F. Minehan
1995 Victor C. Melendy
1996 James A. Ellis
1996 Arthur Petit
1999 Richard C. Bacon
1999 Paul A. Brotherton
1999 Theodore A. Ferrante
1999 Timothy P. Jackson
1999 Jeremiah M. Lucey
1999 James F. Lyons III
1999 Joseph T. McGuirk
1999 John E. Murphy
1999 Joseph R. "Dick" Murphy
1999 David L. Packard
1999 Ronald D. Peters
1999 Thomas E. Spencer
1999 David J. Watts

Michigan Fallen Firefighters

1981 Elmer L. Hodge
1981 Donald C. Graham
1981 George G. Spinner
1981 Coleman A. Tate
1981 Ralph J. Buchman
1981 Frank F. Dailey
1982 Richard N. Boeve
1982 Norman E. Creger
1982 Frank W. Pressey
1982 Richard J. Beer
1983 Edward T. Mosko
1983 James C. Nelson
1983 Gary Kreski

1984 Max D. Nason
1985 Robert Bennett
1985 Bradford C. Lennon
1985 Herbert Rasmussen
1986 William L. Simpson
1987 Larry A. McDonald, Jr.
1987 Richard J. Sugar
1987 Marsha Lee Baczynski
1987 Thomas B. Phelps
1987 Paul W. Schimeck
1987 David W. Lau
1987 Forest C. Flinn
1987 Leonard Gierak
1987 Robert Arnold Gregory, Sr.
1988 Donald L. Riling
1988 Tracy K. Williamson
1988 Paul L. Vanderberg
1988 Gordon Anderson
1989 Stephen L. Waldron
1989 Karl M. Ryan
1989 Christopher A. Hilden
1990 Michael E. VanCalbergh
1990 Richard A. Havens
1991 Joseph Kail
1991 Donald J. Daughenbaugh
1991 Charles Love
1992 Daniel L. Maturen
1992 John A. Navarro
1992 Robert G. Reits, Sr.
1992 Roland Waters
1994 Dennis E. Dearing, Jr.
1994 Robert G. English
1995 John Weingart
1995 Ray D. Tiffany
1995 Bradley E. Hocking
1996 Robert J. Haggadone
1996 Francis Ploeger
1997 James H. Tebo

Roll of Honor

Michigan Fallen Firefighters

1999 Terry T. "Ted" Oliver, Sr.

Minnesota Fallen Firefighters

1982 Bruce J. Raeburn
1982 Marion Cunningham
1982 Richard F. Wagner
1982 Michael E. Kurth
1982 Robert B. Hays
1983 Charles L. Drenth
1984 Thomas K. Hollingsworth
1984 Carl E. Hardel
1985 David J. Kane
1985 Debra R. Swanson
1985 Robert J. Johnson, Jr.
1985 James Hunkins
1985 Victor E. Buckingham
1985 Douglas E. Zabel
1986 John D. Schwenn
1986 Norman A. Lukken
1987 Robert K. Edwards
1989 Daniel J. Wroblewski
1989 Gary L. Skoglund
1989 Larry Dean House
1990 Jerry A. Reed
1991 Frederick W. Templin
1997 LeRoy Swenson
1997 Harvey Jerome Chlian, Jr.
1998 Michael C. "Mick" Wiborg
1999 Marvin Huisman

Mississippi Fallen Firefighters

1982 Archie L. Carouthers

1984 James E. Frazier, Jr.
1985 James A. Whitfield
1985 Ricky E. May
1986 Carl Monroe Ohr
1986 Edwin K. Jacquet
1987 Charles Jerry Schultz, Jr.
1987 Therrell E. Schilling
1988 Danny Lee Claiborne
1988 Tony J. Tadlock
1988 James H. Jackson, Jr.
1989 Paul H. Smith
1989 Henry H. Hinton
1989 Robert P. Hayden
1989 Gerald W. Andresen
1990 Robert Jerry Drennan
1990 Mathe A. Alexander
1991 Nathan E. Walls
1991 James D. Walling
1991 Raymond L. Bryant
1995 Ray Parnell McKay, Jr.
1995 William Dale Luker
1996 W. Dwight Craft
1996 Stanley C. Adams
1996 Meredith "Don" Moree
1996 John "Rick" Robbins
1997 Gerald Ertle
1997 Sam Smitherman
1998 Paula Bennett
1998 Justin Allen Melton
1998 Timothy Selby
1999 David Zan Lancaster
1999 Carl A. Olsen

Missouri Fallen Firefighters

1981 Dale J. Walker
1981 Joseph P. Ritter, Jr.
1981 Henry J. Hoover
1981 Robert M. Edwards

Roll of Honor

Missouri Fallen Firefighters

1982 Garry D. Munn
1982 Kevin L. Blevins
1983 William E. Booth, I
1983 Leonard J. Farr
1983 Richard D. Dixson
1984 Ronald G. Mullins
1984 William R. Smart, Jr.
1985 Glen L. Ussery
1985 John A. Wysong
1985 Kenneth E. Ferguson
1986 George A. Glenn, Sr.
1986 Donald Gene Crum
1987 Earl Dean Koehn
1987 Dwayne VonBehren
1988 Thomas M. Fry
1988 Dennis W. Krause
1988 Robert D. McKarnin
1988 Robert E. Grove
1988 Michael R. Oldham
1988 James H. Kilventon
1988 Gerald C. Halloran
1988 Luther E. Hurd
1988 David Ray Youngblood
1989 Gerard O. Haenni
1989 Ralph S. Burns
1990 James David Straub
1991 Randall P. McDonald
1992 Bryan L. Weeks
1994 David J. Mosher
1994 Gary K. King
1994 Nick J. Charmello
1994 Marcus E. Carr
1995 William Walls
1996 Norman Kenneth Manka
1997 Harold H. Hester, Jr.
1997 David E. Carpenter

1997 Donald Joseph Payton, Sr.
1998 Ralph Wm. Stanbery
1999 Alan William Ducheck
1999 Arthur J. Heckman
1999 Bryan Pottberg
1999 Jeffrey S. Thompson
1999 John H. Tvedten, Jr.

Montana Fallen Firefighters

1981 Donald J. James
1983 Lawrence H. Huber
1988 Patrick Francis David
1988 Cheryl Old Horn Deputee
1989 William J. Weber
1989 Kevin Yeager
1992 Corey R. Clawson
1994 Randy C. Lynn
1994 Robert Eugene Kelly
1994 Donald K. Mackey

Nebraska Fallen Firefighters

1981 Harley G. Grasmick
1982 Robert R. Gardner
1982 Arnold H. Hansen
1983 Barney E. Conley
1984 Patricia Beran
1985 Erwin N. Sample
1987 Willis Edward Leyden
1989 John A. Wilcox
1990 Gene Keith Copple
1993 Francis M. Nichols
1994 Ronald V. Carlson
1996 John P. Goessling
1996 Vinton LeRoy Durflinger
1997 William W. "Bill" Babka
1999 Charles J. Vodak

Roll of Honor

Nevada Fallen Firefighters

1983 Keith L. Lemmons
1986 Billie D. Combs
1987 Maggie M. Durham
1989 Michael V. Copple
1994 Stanley M. Rhoads
1995 Adam Sorenson
1995 John C. Dorff
1996 John Gray

New Hampshire Fallen Firefighters

1981 James A. Taylor
1985 Burton M. Bowen
1987 Marc L. Bechard
1987 Maurice Benwell
1987 Lawrence G. Carbonneau
1987 Bruce Tarpley
1988 Edward D. Gay
1992 Earle V. Dudley, III
1992 David K. Lumbra
1993 Loren E. Baker

New Jersey Fallen Firefighters

1981 Charles Rogallosky
1981 Thomas L. Kernusz
1981 Henry E. Runco
1982 John W. Franklin, Sr.
1983 Charles A. Crowley, Jr.
1983 John J. Thompson
1983 Robert Wasner
1983 Robert P. Cogan
1983 William D. Entwistle
1983 Frederick A. Steffen
1984 James J. Carbin, Jr.
1984 John E. Lindquist, Sr.

1984 Michael W. Thorne
1984 James M. Murray
1985 Leon Dudak
1985 William J. Koenemund
1985 Marinus P. Witte
1985 Marcus A. Reddick
1986 Albert Fischer
1986 Joseph F. Woods, Jr.
1986 John A. Rose
1986 Walter A. Lukaszewski
1986 Howard A. Cooper
1986 Frank Biancorosso
1986 Robert J. Mizopalko
1987 Gerald E. Crowell
1987 Joseph C. Pezzullo
1987 Joseph McCormick, Sr.
1987 John T. Durfee
1987 Gustave H. Dirner, Jr.
1987 Francis X. Tiewski
1987 William J. O'Donnell
1988 Leonard Radumski
1988 Clifford W. Brown
1988 Richard L. Williams
1988 Richard R. Reinhagen
1988 Robert J. Mazzo, Sr.
1988 William Krejsa
1988 Eugene T. Furey
1988 Maurice Frey
1988 Atwood T. Fox III
1988 Stephen H. Ennis
1988 William R. Schmidt
1989 Robert J. Ansell
1989 Dennis J. Haycock
1989 Ray H. Rufe
1989 Louis N. Simone
1989 Eddie A. Jones, Jr.
1990 George S. Labance
1991 Frank A. Quadrel
1991 John A. Nicosia

Roll of Honor

New Jersey Fallen Firefighters

1991 Joseph P. McCarthy
1991 John Kucich
1991 Albert F. Robibero
1992 Anthony J. Carugno
1993 John H. Somay
1993 Russell T. Newcomb
1993 Carlos A. Negron
1993 John Brentzel, Jr.
1993 Lewis R. Sheats
1994 Richard A. Liddy
1994 Walter Franks
1994 Thomas E. Dunn
1994 Michael Jude Delane
1994 George A. Ciliberto
1994 Brian D. Sutton, Sr.
1994 Glenn T. Thorn
1995 Michael Canonico
1995 Peter E. Borwegen
1995 Henry Williams
1996 Leslie Hendricks
1996 Bruce Lindner
1996 Kevin Robert Malone
1996 Michael McLaughlin
1996 Willard R. Hopler
1997 Johnson "Jack" Oatman
1997 Thomas P. Ryan
1998 Walter Bitner
1998 Stephen E. Gessler
1999 Richard A. Heinze
1999 Robert Stanmire
1999 Joseph F. Tagliareni, Jr.

New Mexico Fallen Firefighters

1981 James H. Hockett
1982 James A. Brown

1982 Atilano Fernandez
1983 Edwin S. Irwin
1983 Arthur E. Gurule
1985 Richard Lee Gustafson
1987 Nathan Kolb
1987 Woodard Miller
1989 Ernie Cachini
1989 Travis Eugene Bird
1991 Henry Y. H. Kim
1993 Frankie Toledo
1994 Anthony Sean Gutierrez
1994 Sam H. McCarty, III
1994 Robert G. Boomer
1994 Samuel C. Smith
1995 Ernestine Garcia
1997 Timothy Wayne Martin
1998 Juan Manuel Hernandez, Jr.
1999 Gregory Edwin Pacheco

New York Fallen Firefighters

1981 John P. McGuire
1981 Ronald F. Coates
1981 Robert Reed
1981 Alan F. Hogancamp
1981 William T. Nixon
1981 James E. Devlin
1981 Francis J. Novak
1981 Ralph J. Osterhout
1981 Robert E. Costa
1981 Dennis M. Peterson
1981 Marshall E. Wells
1981 Richard J. Smith
1981 Charles R. Haas
1982 Ronald G. Bazoge
1982 Gary G. Partridge
1982 Charles K. Palmore
1982 Anthony Leogrande

Roll of Honor

New York Fallen Firefighters

1982 Alfred M. Knecht	1984 John C. Huss
1982 Andrew W. Harcher, Jr.	1984 James Jimenez
1982 Barry N. Brown	1984 Frank J. Nerney
1982 Kenneth L. Smith	1985 Charles D. Pickard
1982 Albert F. Fischer	1985 David D. Duncan, Jr.
1982 Donald R. Conklin	1985 Harry Sauer
1982 Robert J. Cahill	1985 Frank DiSarlo
1982 Thomas E. Secovnie, Jr.	1985 Raymond J. Whalen
1983 Anthony Waszkielewicz	1985 Claude Gowdy
1983 Andrew S. Usyk, Sr.	1985 Frank Jelley
1983 Donald R. Bogash	1985 James F. McDonnell
1983 Lawrence E. Miller	1985 C. Clifford Preisigke, III
1983 Alan E. Jones	1985 Edward M. Supples
1983 Michael G. Catanzaro	1985 Leon I. Walton
1983 Arthur L. Cassell, Jr.	1986 Bernard J. Spillman
1983 Leonard J. Bloodgood	1986 David J. Clapp
1983 Michael L. Austin	1986 Edward J. Duggan
1983 Mathew E. Colpoys	1986 Sean P. McGuire
1983 Ernest A. Duquette	1986 Joseph J. McNally, Sr.
1983 Keith Farr	1986 Joseph Minore
1983 Edmund A. Chrosniak	1986 Stephen T. Wade
1983 William N. Hammond	1986 Louis P. Pellegrino
1983 Garry S. Kuehner	1986 Paul P. Shannon
1983 Glenn E. McCoog	1986 Walter J. Borek
1983 James C. Lickfeld	1987 Merle E. Lewis
1983 William J. Ford	1987 John U. Green
1984 Anthony Shands	1987 John J. Toomey
1984 Harry M. Korwatch	1987 Ronald W. Svoboda, Jr.
1984 Robert C. Ayers	1987 Howard E. Scroger
1984 John L. Carlson	1987 Carmen Russo
1984 Kevin J. Cioffi	1987 J. Robert Hickey
1984 Phillip C. D'Adamo	1987 Ernest J. Kane
1984 Mitchel E. Spoth	1987 Earl John Garrity, II
1984 David F. Murry	1987 Louis J. Flury
1984 Russell H. Dixon	1987 Joseph P. Faughnan
1984 Epifanio J. Gonzalez	1987 Robert Cassidy
1984 Ralph E. Hager, Jr.	1987 Samuel D. Carbone
	1987 Anthony N. Capozzi
	1987 Peter J. Canelli

Roll of Honor

New York Fallen Firefighters

1987 Christopher A. Bilger
1988 Robert H. Dayton
1988 Thomas J. Mahoney
1988 Donald R. Henry
1988 Julius C. Greene
1988 Robert L. Goodrich, Sr.
1988 Michael D. Gerrie
1988 Clyde W. Miller
1988 Oscar F. Dell
1988 Edward Stanczyk
1988 Robert Francis Cushing
1988 James P. Cummins
1988 William J. Cruickshank
1988 Duane F. Ahl
1988 Howard Garrison
1988 William H. Smith
1988 Roger D. Snyder
1989 Lawrence R. Smith, Sr.
1989 John P. Devaney
1989 Frank M. Hausauer
1989 Theodore W. Hilsinger
1989 Donald Hilton
1989 Daniel C. Strong
1989 Donald M. Hodgkinson
1989 Michael Moschenross
1989 Ernest Smith
1989 Norman J. Rowe
1989 William Sinzer
1989 Colin Fell
1989 Dominic A. Lagudi, Jr.
1989 Donald J. Smith
1989 Thomas Razzano
1990 Karl Richter
1990 George J. Karl
1990 William F. Carter, Sr.
1990 Bruce A. Rhinehart
1990 Dale M. Seib

1990 Edwin Simpson
1990 Ingrid H. Sowle
1990 Paul Edward Caywood, Sr.
1990 Robert L. Hitchcock
1990 Daniel R. Joslyn
1990 John L. Kelley, Jr.
1991 Edward W. Murdock
1991 Scott T. Laverty
1991 Gregory E. Williams
1991 Joseph Farrell
1991 Kevin C. Kane
1991 Russell E. Dunham
1991 Gordon O. Schmidt
1991 Alfred E. Ronaldson
1991 Eugene Miller
1991 Daniel J. Miller, Jr.
1991 William H. Marshall, Jr.
1991 Robert J. Lucier, Sr.
1991 Marshall F. Sarles
1991 Joseph R. Bow
1991 Alston F. Hill, Sr.
1991 Randolph F. Belcher
1991 Brian T. Dillon
1992 Thomas A. Williams
1992 John C. Nelson, Jr.
1992 Arthur K. Tuck
1992 Harold J. Lyons, Sr.
1992 Frank L. Schips, Jr.
1993 Dennis Rodd
1993 Christopher P. Savage
1993 Richard E. Gleason, Sr.
1993 Gary L. Kennicutt
1993 Charles H. Beadle
1993 Norman G. Schunk, Jr.
1993 Ronald L. O'Rourke
1993 Howard R. Schmitt, Sr.
1993 Richard Beck
1993 Patrick Lafferty

Roll of Honor

New York Fallen Firefighters

1993 Warren R. Ogburn
1993 Dale E. Linkroum
1993 Vincent D. Meegan, Jr.
1994 John J. Drennan
1994 Christopher J.
Siedenburg
1994 Wayne E. Smith
1994 Thomas A. Wylie
1994 James F. Young
1994 Elias Ovsiovitch
1994 Dwight G. Burger, Jr.
1994 Gerald F. Mullins
1994 Paul A. MacMurray
1994 James Harris, Jr.
1994 Joseph D. Jarvis, Sr.
1994 Dennis J. Mullins, Jr.
1994 George W. Lener
1994 Gerald E. Murray
1995 Neil Hyland
1995 Frederick T. Fairweather
1995 Walter Augustyn
1995 John M. Clancy
1995 James Weaver
1995 John Woodard
1995 June Fitzpatrick
1995 Peter F. McLaughlin
1995 John Francis Pache, Sr.
1995 Raymond F. Schiebel
1995 Stephen Sulzinski
1995 Kevin Sutch
1995 Arthur Thompson
1995 James Dworetsky
1996 Thomas Dorr, Sr.
1996 Louis Valentino, Jr.
1996 Donald A. Collins
1996 James B. Williams
1996 Walter J. Schwinger, Jr.

1996 Karl A. Schmidt
1996 Guy Pollard
1996 Rex E. Hoad
1996 Albert DeFlumere
1997 Albert W. Sippel
1997 Michael Neuner, Sr.
1997 Kevin C. Seaburg
1997 Michael L. Seguin
1997 Edwin J. Haungs, Sr.
1997 Leonard N. Zeller
1997 Timothy Michael Goff
1997 William H. Fairweather
1997 Brian D. Myers, Sr.
1997 Thomas M. McCormack
1997 H. Peter Kahn
1997 Timothy J. Warren, III
1997 Robert E. Fowler
1997 John F. Kroening
1998 James W. Blackmore
1998 James F. Bohan
1998 Christopher Michael
Bopp
1998 Joseph P. Cavalieri
1998 Walter A. Ernst
1998 Scott J. LaPiedra
1998 Edward J. Matter, Jr.
1998 Daniel W. Mumford
1998 Raymond Nakovics
1998 Robert F. Peters
1998 Thomas B. Rice
1998 William J. Robertson
1998 Harold "Hal" E. Roemer,
Jr.
1998 Lawrence D. Thrower
1999 Kenneth F. Clinch
1999 Vincent G. Fowler
1999 William Korte
1999 Alton L. Lewis
1999 James H. McGroarty

Roll of Honor

New York Fallen Firefighters

1999 Dan O'Connell
1999 Wayne S. Rosen
1999 Jerome Taylor

*North Carolina Fallen
Firefighters*

1981 Robert M. Wynn
1981 Merton R. Jackson
1981 Hampton L. Hobbs
1982 Gregory M. Lamm
1982 Raymond J. Flowers
1982 Asa T. Squires
1982 James F. Spry, Sr.
1982 Jesse M. Woolard, Jr.
1982 James L. Harris
1983 John C. Tyner, Sr.
1983 David F. Cook
1984 Russell C. Dellinger, Sr.
1984 William G. Countiss
1984 Robert B. Gamble
1984 Max L. Daniel
1985 Dwight W. Dabbs
1986 Rayford D. Coston
1986 Ferrell D. Hood
1986 Paul E. Farmer
1986 James A. Beshears
1987 Brian K. Rodgers
1987 Harold Lee Sandlin
1988 Franklin W. Winslow
1988 Steve E. Russell, Jr.
1989 Sammie J. Waddell
1989 Timothy P. Bennett
1989 Erwin Derke
1989 Grover C. Brinkley
1989 Roy Lee Bailey
1990 Ronnie E. Hoots

1990 Charles Ray Lowery, II
1991 James Hugh Lee
1992 Michael D. Hoover
1993 Patrick J. Dougherty
1994 Jesse U. Shockley, Jr.
1994 Jake Parris, Jr.
1995 James Clyde Shue
1995 James Gregg Hinson
1996 George Michael Guyer
1996 Richard C. "Rick" Dorsey
1996 Leonard W. Coulter
1997 Henry Ernest Perry
1998 Robby Dean Blizzard
1998 Brian Allen Cannon
1998 Carson Lee Gosey
1998 Hubert Sidney Jones
1999 Kenneth Alan Strain

*North Dakota Fallen
Firefighters*

1984 Jeffrey L. Haugen
1991 Craig W. Keith
1992 Kevin Johnson

Ohio Fallen Firefighters

1981 Donnie G. Cathcart
1981 Richard A. Eierdam
1981 Richard L. Yarman
1981 Eugene F. Jankowski
1981 Lawrence J. Hauserman
1982 Phillip S. Kibler
1982 Maurice Gates
1982 Frank I. McMannes
1982 Earl R. Shelton
1982 Lawrence D. Savage
1983 Richard D. Shively
1983 Robert W. Raitz, Sr.

Roll of Honor

Ohio Fallen Firefighters

1983 Dale F. Eyerdom
1983 Bruce E. Mettler
1983 Raymond C. Hickman
1983 Michael L. Sweeney
1983 Duane F. Dress
1984 Robert G. Chilcote II
1984 James B. Daniels
1984 John W. Walsh
1985 Tommy J. Ware
1985 Robert K. Galehouse
1985 Daniel R. Pescatrice
1985 Edward L. Brillhart
1986 Albert P. Dingle
1986 James N. Eddy
1986 Arthur J. Girty
1986 William Bryan Gray, Sr.
1986 Ray E. Scott
1986 Orval Jean Steele
1986 Harold Wayne Seek
1986 Edgar J. Schneider
1987 Raymond D. Holtz
1987 John W. Nance
1988 Arnold E. Weaver
1988 Frank E. McGaffick
1988 Robert W. Leas
1988 James E. Harvey, Jr.
1988 Patrick E. Yahle
1989 John A. Rozzi, Jr.
1989 Ricke E. Phillips
1990 John J. Meyer
1991 Brooks Cowgill
1991 Thomas E. Coyne, Jr.
1991 Kinnison F. Cribley
1991 Arthur R. Denny, II
1991 Jennifer L. Kibbey
1992 Roy J. Swinehart
1992 Arthur E. Schumacher

1993 Brian E. Metts
1993 F. Allan Coates
1993 Donald C. Cottrell
1994 Michael P. Shaughnessy
1994 Timothy S. J. Shiltz
1994 Earl G. Detty, Jr.
1994 Dale E. Nelboeck
1994 Walter E. Wade
1995 Edward Carey
1995 Ronald Fogel
1995 John McCroden
1996 Henry L. Scott
1996 Jeffrey K. Renner
1996 Terry Leasher
1997 Charles A. Rudd
1997 Kathryn Ann Mayfield
1997 Arthur R. Ebert
1997 Robert Douglas Good
1997 James H. Johnson
1998 Stephen D. Carletti
1998 Robert J. O'Toole
1998 David Paul Theisen
1999 Kenneth C. Cashman
1999 Michael E. Cupp, Sr.
1999 Brad A. Michener
1999 Gregory E. Rodgers

Oklahoma Fallen Firefighters

1981 Zappy C. Ott
1981 Stanley M. Bumgarner
1982 Preston Arnold
1982 James O. Lee
1982 Johnnie F. Jackson
1983 Harold L. Baker
1985 Alvie L. Hudgens
1985 Jimmie A. McElwain
1985 Guy T. Cooper
1986 Robert E. Smith

Roll of Honor

Oklahoma Fallen Firefighters

1989 Jefferey N. Lindsay
1989 Jimmy L. Ayers
1989 Arnold Leo Glenn, Jr.
1989 Billy G. Warren
1989 Steven W. Begley
1989 Sonny Bevard
1989 Bennie D. Zellner
1990 Edward P. Dougherty, Jr.
1990 Ronald L. Stroud
1992 George William Ousley
1994 Dustin Lee Sample Mills
1994 Marilyn K. Williams
1994 Gus E. Fullbright, Jr.
1994 Charles Dee Butchee
1996 Bill Vinson
1996 Mathew B. Hatcher
1996 Marvin Mathes, Jr.
1996 Nathaniel E. Quinn, Sr.
1997 Thomas C. Reynolds
1998 Timothy D. Allen
1998 Warren Dee Myers, Jr.
1999 James E. Clark III
1999 Jack Garnett

Oregon Fallen Firefighters

1981 Paul F. Yost
1982 Robert W. Thompson
1982 Michael K. Maine
1982 Clyde E. Golden
1984 Richard H. Bowers
1984 David C. Stephens
1984 Elwin I. King
1984 Barbara A. Booth
1985 Mary L. Francis
1986 Michael Allen Lehman
1987 Russell Brine

1988 Joseph J. Stroda
1988 Wendell L. Beck
1988 Louis A. Mohr
1988 David Alfred Schas
1989 William D. Mills
1990 Julius C. Starr
1990 William McAdams
1992 James Shannon
        Campbell
1993 Brian L. Hill
1994 Scott A. Blecha
1994 Tamera Jean Bickett
1994 Kathi Julie Beck
1994 Levi J. Brinkley
1994 Jon Roy Kelso
1994 Bonnie Jean Holtby
1994 Robert Alan Johnson
1994 Sydney B. Maplesden
1994 Douglas Michael Dunbar
1994 Terri Ann Hagen
1995 Phillip Sherburn
1995 Henry Walter Howe
1997 Robert Chisholm
1998 George Converse

*Pennsylvania Fallen
Firefighters*

1981 William E. Moss
1981 Donald L. Myers
1981 Frederick Mantz
1981 Joseph C. Sella
1981 Gordon D. Stark, Sr.
1981 Charles B. Zeigler
1981 John G. Heidish
1981 Robert C. Harpster
1981 John R. Buchner
1981 Edward C. Rupp
1981 Paul E. Ahrens

Roll of Honor

Pennsylvania Fallen Firefighters

1981 Jeffrey W. Jones
1981 Thomas G. Cagni
1982 Grant E. Morrow
1982 Patrick L. Bowman
1982 Leroy A. Harris
1982 Donald C. Geckle
1982 Wilbur E. Stough
1982 William C. Wardlaw
1982 Earl J. Carnahan
1982 Joseph P. Czerw
1982 James A. Fogle
1982 Kenneth M. Gallagher
1982 Fred V. Kleinfelter
1983 Hilbert J. Reiner
1983 Gregory A. Stauffer
1983 Joseph D. Arnold, Sr.
1983 Robert F. Spangenberg
1983 Erich J. Buzilow, II
1983 Erick D. Fitzgerald
1983 Frederick W. Mayberry
1983 Richard C. Miller
1983 Leon Morris
1983 Donald P. Semyon
1983 Harvey C. Wolf
1984 Anthony J. Lundy, Sr.
1984 Julian R. Bley, Sr.
1984 Joseph L. Konrad, Jr.
1984 Charles J. Elder
1984 David A. DeWire
1984 John P. Brighenti, Jr.
1984 Joseph Somma
1985 Jack Greer
1985 Robert Binder
1985 John J. Durco, Sr.
1985 John C. Edwards
1985 Thomas J. Gibson

1985 Vernon H. Harmon
1985 Katherine M. Hippensteel
1985 Donald G. Jacobs
1985 Carmen A. Lettieri
1985 Francis C. Lewis
1985 John F. Moore
1985 Frank Poatsy
1985 H. Gordon Walker
1985 Phillip R. Eicke
1986 Brinton C. Moyer
1986 Stanley R. Konefal, Sr.
1986 Carl E. Bird, Sr.
1986 Edward D. Friel
1986 Harry J. Henz
1986 Herbert J. Pinkowicz
1986 John W. Tuttle
1986 Vincent H. Eckrote
1987 Dennis J. Briggs, Sr.
1987 Park Wagenbach
1987 Thomas E. Probst
1987 Darryl W. Fultz
1987 Fred Ferraino, Jr.
1987 Charles James Deal
1987 Kenneth E. Steel
1988 Milton E. Major
1988 Michael G. Macik
1988 Jack E. Jones
1988 Lawrence E. Greeley
1988 John W. Fry
1988 Thomas P. Foy, Jr.
1988 Charles B. Danylo
1988 Calvin A. Beam
1988 Robert W. Miller
1988 Kenneth J. Cara
1988 Tom H. Blessing, Jr.
1988 Michael R. Rozick
1988 Robert Z. Seaman
1988 James M. Stevens

Roll of Honor

Pennsylvania Fallen
Firefighters

1988 Charles O. Wehlage
1988 Harold F. Beck, Jr.
1988 John J. Opiary, Jr.
1989 Richard W. Roberts
1989 Richard B. Tucholski
1989 Robert Huffert
1989 James Brian Harnly
1989 Paul K. Frederick
1989 Harry D. Hess
1989 William H. Schell, Sr.
1989 John J. Slezak
1989 David E. Martino
1990 Thomas N. Bianconi
1990 Mark A. Wunch
1990 Robert L. Adams, Sr.
1990 James F. Chesnut, Jr.
1990 Fred R. Garber
1990 Frederick J. Heimann, Jr.
1990 Willard C. Kuhns
1990 Thomas L. Lane
1990 Timothy M. Stine
1990 Richard L. Hershey
1991 Edward E. Soper
1991 David G. Emanuelson
1991 Michael J. Cielicki Burns
1991 James A. Chappell
1991 Stephen D. Yale
1991 John G. Dugan
1991 Charles H. Boyle
1991 Richard A. Frantz
1991 David P. Holcombe
1991 George Hollowniczky
1991 Phyllis McAllister
1991 Daniel Glenn Paris
1991 Albert R. Smith
1991 Frank Veri, Jr.

1992 Thomas J. Horvath
1992 Guy C. Miller
1992 Nelson Margerum
1992 Charles E. Fierson
1992 Victor E. Eager
1992 Robert D. Barnes
1992 James W. Schott
1992 Raymond E. Talley
1993 Joseph D. DelVecchio, Sr.
1993 John F. Lombardo
1993 Harry B. Garis
1993 Richard A. Hartley
1993 Joseph A. Hummel
1993 Joseph E. Kozlowski
1993 Arthur Karr
1993 Leonard C. Insalaco, II
1994 Vencent C. Acey
1994 Victor John Ruth, III
1994 John J. Redmond
1995 John Schuyler
1995 George Peters
1995 Thomas A. Brooks
1995 Eric L. Mangieri
1995 Patricia Ann Conroy
1995 John Fisher
1995 Marc R. Kolenda
1995 William Marks
1996 William Robert Favinger, Sr.
1996 John Russell Bryant
1996 William A. Frank
1996 Kris Wesley Sherman
1996 Reed E. Morton, Sr.
1996 Walter L. Bricker
1997 Harold E. McGowan
1997 William H. "Pop" Winters
1997 Carl L. Ayers
1997 James E. Hynes
1997 George Hopey, Jr.

Roll of Honor

Pennsylvania Fallen Firefighters

1997 Scott Alan Vrabel
1997 David A. Womer
1997 McClay Watson
1997 Joseph M. Vagnier
1997 Terry K. McElveen
1998 Thomas J. Concannon
1998 David J. Good
1998 Calvin Harbaugh, Sr.
1998 Stephen E. Murphy
1998 Douglas L. Rohrbaugh
1998 Barry L. Wary
1999 Eric Noel Casiano
1999 Philip P. Cirrito
1999 Richard F. Devine
1999 Larry D. Lehman
1999 Paul F. McGrath
1999 Michael J. Sims, Sr.
1999 Walter F. Vaughan
1999 Frank W. Wood
1999 Wayne C. Yost

Puerto Rico Fallen Firefighters

1998 Jesus Garcia
1998 Luis A. Rivera

Rhode Island Fallen Firefighters

1983 Peter J. D'Abrosca
1986 Lawrence F. Gingell, Sr.
1992 Chester F. Warner
1992 William N. Jones, Jr.
1992 Loyd Horton, Jr.
1993 John F. Hargreaves
1994 Harold L. Salisbury

1997 Ronald Albert Guilmette

South Carolina Fallen Firefighters

1981 William E. Goude
1981 Roger B. Casselman
1982 Foster C. Brandon
1982 Perry Crowley
1984 George Kuharsky
1985 Richard E. Webb
1985 James T. Flanagan
1985 Vernon W. Gaines
1985 Ozakie B. Knotts
1985 Francis W. Sheppard
1985 Gilbert Wiggins
1986 John J. Rhodes, Sr.
1986 Warren F. Morris, Jr.
1986 John M. Barry
1986 Randy S. Branch
1987 Frank Hut
1987 Strother D. Paysinger, Jr.
1987 Benjamin Ryans, Jr.
1987 Thomas H. Brown
1987 Terry L. Dobbins
1988 John L. Headrick
1988 Ray A. Hayes
1988 Homer M. Cook
1989 Adell R. Potts
1990 Anthony L. Boyert
1990 Robert Edward Lee
1991 Robert Dale Morris, II
1991 Jerry Brooks
1993 James Rhett LaFon
1994 Robert E. Browning, Jr.
1994 Ronnie M. Fuller
1995 Thomas B. Buff, Jr.
1995 Jimmy Bryant
1996 Jack Lloyd Capps

Roll of Honor

South Carolina Fallen
Firefighters

1996 Lee A. Steele
1996 Ronald Bryan Lupo
1996 Monty Jason Harmon
1998 Randel Neal "Randy"
     Sims
1999 Lewis E. Anderson
1999 Timmy Rogers Dawson
1999 Aubrey R. Tillman, Jr.

South Dakota Fallen
Firefighters

1988 Richard L. McDonald
1988 Wayne T. Schlosser
1991 Curtis D. Mikkelsen

Tennessee Fallen Firefighters

1981 Archie C. Reed
1981 William H. Shields
1981 Earl R. Harrison
1982 Ricky L. Hitchcox
1982 J. Wendall Organ
1982 Charles H. Vinson
1983 Thomas Girdley
1984 Milton A. Densford
1984 Jimmy R. Kennedy
1984 Willis D. Fry
1985 James L. Craig, Jr.
1986 Carl A. Bettis, Jr.
1986 Robert K. Bell
1987 Robert O. Binkley
1987 James Clayton George
1987 Bobby Gene Blackley
1988 George Harold Carathers,
     Sr.

1988 Charles J. Berry
1988 Alex J. Sparks
1989 David Ellis Pratt
1989 David A. McCollum
1989 Eddie D. Diviney
1990 Robbie Davis
1991 James T. Swindle
1992 James D. Hill
1992 Joseph A. Boswell
1993 Mark R. Hinson, Sr.
1994 Michael L. Mathis
1994 Edward L. Freeman
1994 Dwight E. Smith
1994 William E. Bridges
1995 Gene Schubert
1995 Wilbur Pinnell
1995 Corey Berggren
1995 Ronnie Wilson
1995 Henry Frizzell
1996 W. Clark Derryberry
1997 Tracy D. Floyd
1997 William Thomas Wilson
1997 Scott M. Berry
1998 Larry Joe King, Sr.

Texas Fallen Firefighters

1981 William C. Dale
1981 W. Bruce Fiedling
1981 Charles L. Metters
1981 Charles R. Rogers, Jr.
1982 R. L. Walker, Sr.
1982 Thomas M. Cooper
1982 Virgil Pace
1982 Leo Spicer, Jr.
1982 Kenneth A. Caldwell
1982 Charles L. Smith
1983 Herman R. Tidwell
1983 Lonnie L. Franklin

Roll of Honor

Texas Fallen Firefighters

1984 Larry D. Stephens
1984 Jeffrey A. Hardin
1984 Elmer Homilius
1984 Keith A. Norman
1984 James E. Pressnall
1984 Robert M. Reyes
1984 Marvin B. Ridgway
1984 James C. Simpson
1984 Earl W. Walker
1984 Thomas C. Ross
1985 Paul M. Hand
1985 Michael F. West
1985 Kenneth C. Whitney
1985 Louis Kunde, Jr.
1985 Robert L. Keen
1985 Hilario Bustos
1985 Barry J. Hawthorne
1985 Benny M. Gracy
1985 Larry D. Gartner
1985 Adam M. Tucker
1985 Ronald B. Snow
1985 Jesse Y. Lara
1986 Charles R. Frederick, Sr.
1986 Vergil L. Cavin
1986 Charles T. Richardson
1986 John W. Savage
1986 James H. Combs
1987 Vandell Weathers
1987 Merwin P. Weitzel
1987 James R. Allen, Sr.
1987 Adrian R. Cal
1987 Ernesto A. Flores
1987 Bennie F. Killion
1987 Dale W. Rhine
1988 Stanley McDonnough
1988 Clint D. Christians
1988 John Mason Miller

1988 Doris G. Hale
1989 Gaylon G. Smith
1989 Cecil Robey Lovett
1989 Lannie E. Hatton
1989 Talmadge O. Fulce
1989 Billy Wayne Bass
1989 Roland D. Lambert
1989 Billy Ross Brooks
1989 Michael G. McAdams
1990 Edgar Dear
1990 Ronnie Michael
      McAndrew
1990 Leonard E. Mills, Sr.
1990 Lydia A. Sexton
1990 James Earl White
1991 Joseph J. Alfred
1991 George R. Whiteside
1992 Roberto Valdez
1992 Tommy A. Parker
1992 Jeffrey G. Osmun
1992 Rebecca Ann LeClaire
1992 Lupe Guerrero
1993 William Grounds
1993 Jimmy L. Jackson
1993 Richard C. McQuaide, Sr.
1994 Clifford R. Harris
1994 Anthony R. Bullard
1994 James L. Certain
1995 Christopher Rezac
1995 David Barrera
1995 Richard A. Hogan
1995 Marcus King
1995 Glenn Irwin Scott
1995 Jared Lee Wright
1995 Joe W. Novosad, Sr.
1996 Ruben Lopez
1996 Lynn Dale Burkhalter
1996 Jerald L. Dibbles
1996 James Alvin Warwick

Roll of Honor

Texas Fallen Firefighters

1996 William R. McGinnis, III
1997 Jessie F. Bricker, Jr.
1998 Barvon Coy Hamilton
1998 Steven C. Mayfield
1998 Patrick Henry McKinney, Jr.
1998 Steve Austin Tippens
1999 William M. Bethune
1999 Bert A. Bruecher
1999 Victor C. Castillo
1999 B.F. Chesnut
1999 Brian W. Collins
1999 Cilton Jay Dauzat
1999 Phillip W. Dean
1999 James M. Dunham
1999 David D. Hartwick
1999 Clyde A. Peterson
1999 Garry Charles Sanders

Utah Fallen Firefighters

1990 Ralph M. Broadhead
1990 Blake V. Wright
1996 Norman J. Ray

Vermont Fallen Firefighters

1981 Terry B. Brown
1981 Dana H. Fuller
1984 Patrick J. DeKramer
1984 David L. Anderson
1984 Matthew R. Baran
1984 Richard M. Barron
1987 David Christopher Winot
1988 Robert B. Costine
1991 Robert L. Parker
1992 Gordon A. Champney

1994 Maurice W. Wardwell, Jr.
1996 Floyd Carl Birchmore
1998 Charles P. Frank
1998 Eugene P. McDonough
1999 Philip M. Pinkowski, Jr.

Virginia Fallen Firefighters

1981 William B. Travis
1981 Larry W. Marks
1981 David A. Cosner
1982 Michael D. Goff
1982 John R. Small, Jr.
1982 William M. Miller
1999 Bradley C. McNeer
1982 Hunter E. Gurley
1983 William J. Mahoney
1984 Calvin C. Garrett
1984 Michael G. Sims
1985 Robert G. Cassell
1985 Thomas Phillips
1985 Frederick G. LeGrys
1985 Harvey H. Helm, Sr.
1985 John W. Askew, Jr.
1985 George H. Knight
1986 Jerrold W. Branch, Sr.
1986 Michael Brian Bassett
1987 Neal W. Conwell
1987 Danny Wayne Morris
1988 Robert L. Hoeflein
1989 James E. Quesenberry
1989 Matthew B. Smith
1989 Jay Mark Miller
1990 Floyd M. Price
1990 Walter J. Scruggs
1990 Robert T. Crutchfield, III
1990 Mark E. Polan
1990 Vernon Dennis Deshazor
1991 Larry H. Brooks

Roll of Honor

Virginia Fallen Firefighters

1991 Lynn E. Maricle
1992 Gwyn L. Ellis
1993 Walter E. Sivertson, Jr.
1993 Samuel Isaac Boyce
1993 David M. Dunkerley
1994 Steven A. Colona
1994 Anthony Covas
1995 Christopher M. Garneau
1995 Carter Martin
1996 Frank Eric Young
1996 John Robert Hudgins, Jr.
1996 Corey Clifton Morgan
1997 John F. Lincoln, Jr.
1997 William S. "Sam"
     Bradner, III
1999 Bradley C. McNeer

*Washington Fallen
  Firefighters*

1981 Julian J. Malek
1981 Ronnie O. Beems
1982 Levy H. Nelson
1982 Paul J. Heidenreich
1982 Edward A. Carbaugh
1982 Raymond H. Kadow
1983 Lisa Long
1984 Mary R. Matthews
1985 Timothy J. Trudell
1985 Jaycee Nosie
1985 James E. Dunlap
1986 Cash L. Hopkins
1986 Daniel R. Lohr
1987 Michael P. Adams
1987 Robert D. Earhart
1987 Gary L. Parks
1988 Jean Verville

1988 Robert R. Sittner
1988 Lincoln McGowan
1989 Ralph W. Boyle
1989 Ron Nelson
1989 Jeannette Dozier
1989 Matthew W. Johnson
1990 Loren Neil Christian
1990 Robert P. Weibe
1990 Ralph F. Glasgow
1990 Stephen E. Bovey
1990 Toni J. Godsil
1992 Paul K. Bjorklund
1994 Paul T. Hodges
1994 John C. King
1995 Randall R. Terlicker
1995 James T. Brown
1995 Gregory A. Shoemaker
1995 Walter D. Kilgore
1995 Dana Morrison
1996 Jonathan Cameron
     Boster
1997 Russett S. "Rusty"
     Hauber
1997 Charlie "JR" Mestaz

*West Virginia Fallen
  Firefighters*

1981 Ernest C. Gregory
1982 Jack Wall
1982 Ernest Walker
1982 Merle Mongold
1982 Harry D. Carney
1983 Harold J. Cornell
1983 James D. Mahaney
1984 James E. Bennett
1985 Donald I. Kemmerer
1986 Stephen D. Chapman
1986 William R. VanGilder

Roll of Honor

West Virginia Fallen Firefighters

1990 Peter Baltic
1990 William P. Grimes
1990 Curtis McClain
1991 Timothy P. Scarbrough
1991 Robert H. Foster, Sr.
1993 Troy V. Henderson
1994 Marc L. Butcher
1995 James Ainsworth
1995 Mitch Weaver
1996 Robert Bibbee
1996 William L. Parsons
1998 Gregory Scott Carter
1998 Robert O. Lee
1999 Arch R. Sligar

Wisconsin Fallen Firefighters

1981 Thomas L. Anderson
1981 Ricky K. Genth
1981 Carl Lackey
1981 Gary C. Soper
1981 Lawrence R. Schampers
1981 James J. Lorbeck
1982 Donald L. Eisberner
1982 Floyd H. Kessler
1982 Wayne C. Lake
1983 Barry V. Johnson
1984 John W. Hofacker
1984 Paul J. Dagenbach
1986 Victor Weinzierl
1986 Bruce E. Hoffman
1986 Arthur Weber
1987 Richard H. Ziemer
1988 Jeffrey J. Burclaw
1989 Harvey J. Ashmore

1989 Charles Robert Mangerson
1990 Richard A. Penning
1991 John A. DuChateau
1992 Dean O. Pucker
1992 Heather D. Dzioba
1993 Gary C. Prueser
1994 Evan Buchholtz
1994 Victor J. Delellis
1994 Lionel L. Hoffer
1994 Robert P. Waskiewicz
1995 Bruce A. Cormican
1996 William J. Zokan
1996 Dennis D. McGarry
1996 Raymond Emmrich
1997 Robert W. Martinson, Sr.
1997 Gregory I. Quinn
1998 Richard L. Kalous

Wyoming Fallen Firefighters

1983 Gene A. Ahrendt
1988 Darrell D. Staley
1988 Steven L. Huitt
1988 Edward L. Hutton
1988 Merrin D. Rodgers
1988 Donald B. Kuykendall
1989 Alan L. Mickelson
1991 James E. Dame
1993 Wilbert F. Hansen
1996 Bruce Allan Honstain
1997 W. John Hirth

Battling the Flames

*A special dedication to all those
who devote their lives to caring for others
in the fire and rescue service.*

A thirst for action that never faded away
    Caused me to be a firefighter today—
Quenching the fires that bring such strife
    Is why serving and protecting is my way of life.

As a child I dreamed at the siren's wail,
    Of times when fires were fought with pails.
Even now, with techniques, 'state of the art',
    Extinguishing the blaze is a matter of heart.

Working a fire is dangerous, then pleasing.
    Dark embers mean the fire is through teasing.

The Heart Behind the Hero

So we break down our gear and go on our way,
  Ready for the next scene where our hoses we'll lay.

The training intense, and experience a must—
  But, just as important, in God we trust.
From the newest ladderman to the seasoned chief,
  Our solemn duty to give our neighbors relief.

Rich with history, the fire service looks to the future
  Knowing a way you can help, even nurture;
Will you find a moment to say a heartfelt prayer
  For those of us concerned with your care?

Timothy Christopher Cummings,
Former elected member of the Houston Fire Museum, Inc.
Board of Trustees
Houston, Texas

Authors & Contributors

We would like to thank all of our authors and contributors for their support and encouragement throughout the production of *The Heart Behind the Hero*. As firefighters and paramedics you are an example of the thoughtful, caring and dedicated people that comprise America's fire and rescue service. With deepest gratitude, we thank you for sharing your heartfelt stories.

Johneen "Jay" Castle has been a firefighter/emergency medical technician with the Alexandria St. Albans Township Fire Department in Alexandria, Ohio, for nine years. She began as a volunteer, and just completed her first year of employment with the department. Johneen also is a hazardous materials technician, juvenile firesetter educator, fire investigator, certified fire safety inspector, and fire prevention educator. She and her husband Rob are both first-generation firefighters raising two sons near Johnstown, Ohio.

Michael R. Chase has been a firefighter/emergency medical technician in Nantucket, Massachusetts since 1989. He carries on a two-hundred-plus year family tradition of service to his community. His uncle, grandfather and great-grandfather, who manned fire brigades in Nantucket during the late 1800s, have all contributed to their hometown in the fire service. Michael's love for fighting fires is only second to his true loves—daughter Meghan and future wife Holly, without whose inspiration he would often find it difficult to work—or write!

Timothy Christopher Cummings was elected to a two year term to the Board of Trustees of the Houston Fire Museum in 1988. He currently serves his community in the Texas State Guard as the Flight Sergeant for the 447th Medical Flight at Ellington Field Air National Guard Base. His poem, *Battling the Flames*, took on a special meaning for him on February 14, 2000, when Houston firefighters Kimberly Smith and Lewis Mayo III were killed in the line of duty. They worked out of Station 76, the firehouse that serves Cummings' neighborhood. You can share your thoughts on *Battling the Flames* by contacting him at chris.cummings@txsgair.org.

James M. Ellis began his fire service career in September, 1977. He functioned as a volunteer firefighter and industrial firefighter before becoming a full time career firefighter. Jim has been with the Costa Mesa Fire Department in California since February, 1980. He served as firefighter, firefighter/paramedic, training captain, suppression captain and, currently, battalion chief. He developed and implemented an honor guard program for the CMFD, which has functioned in fire service events across the United States. He has also given back to the fire service by teaching firefighters since 1984. Jim loves the fire service and, as his wife Debbie always says, "became a firefighter for all the right reasons." His prayer is that God will protect and watch over his vast *fire family.*

Doug Faulisi of Schenectady, New York, has been a professional firefighter for twenty-six years. Everyday he thanks the Lord for giving him the opportunity to do something he loves so much. He has two grown boys—Brian is a teacher, and Dougie also is a fireman—working out of the same station as his dad! That is another story in itself! Doug has been married to Margie for sixteen years and feels very blessed to have a close family and wonderful career.

Marc. D. Greenwood is a twenty-year veteran of the Akron Fire Department in Akron, Ohio, having served as lieutenant for the last nine years. Marc is a CPR instructor and paramedic, and currently pursuing a Fire Science Degree. Marc is married to Deborah Greenwood. Together, they have four sons.

Dary Matera is the co-author of *Angels of Emergency* and the author of nine additional books, including *Childlight, Quitting the Mob, Taming the Beast, What's In It For Me?,* and the *New York Times* bestseller *Are You Lonesome Tonight?* His books and subjects have been featured on *20/20, 48 Hours, 60 Minutes, A Current Affair, Donahue, Expose, Good Morning America, Hollywood Insider, Inside Edition, Larry King Live, Nightline, Oprah, Personalities, PM Magazine, Primetime Live, Regis and Kathy Lee, The E True Hollywood Story,* and more. Matera, 45, was formerly a reporter for *The Miami News* and worked as an editor in the book division of *Rodale Press*, the publishers of *Prevention* magazine. At *Rodale*, he was responsible for writing and editing selected chapters in six health and fitness books with sales of more than four million.

Jon McDuffie has been a firefighter with the Los Angeles City Fire Department for twelve years. Jon is a third generation political activist and works as a speechwriter for those seeking elected office. Jon and his wife Suzanne, a police officer with the LAPD, live in Long Beach, California. You can e-mail Jon at mcduffie@earthlink.net.

Tim Miller joined Alabama's Saginaw Fire Department in 1996 at the age of 42, without prior experience. He became an EMT-basic in early 1997, EMT-intermediate in 1999, and working toward becoming a Medic by the end of 2000. Patricia, Tim's wife, serves on the fire board in their community. Together, they have two daughters. April and Alison. April, the oldest daughter, became an EMT at seventeen. She also is a member of the Saginaw Fire Department. Being an ex-professional musician, Tim loves music, movies, the fire department, and his old and newly rejuvenated hobby of vacuum electronics.

Tommy Neiman is a sixteen-year veteran firefighter/
paramedic. His department, St. Lucie county Fire-
Rescue, has been featured on *Rescue 911* three times
and he is the author of *Sirens for the Cross*. Tommy
also is an ordained pastor. He inspires many by traveling throughout the country as an inspirational
speaker.

Patricia Rannigan is the wife of David Rannigan, a
Norfolk, Virginia firefighter since 1977. David serves as
a Hazardous Material Specialist with the Norfolk Fire
and Paramedical Services. Patricia has written a
collection of inspirational poems from her experiences
and perspective as a firefighter's wife. "Silent Alarm" is
one of three poems from her collection that was dis-
played at the Inaugural Memorial Service for Fallen
Firefighters in Hampton Roads, on February 13, 2000.
David and Patricia reside in Chesapeake, Virginia,
where they raise their son.

Sue Reynolds is a writer, speaker, former educator,
and co-author of *Sirens for the Cross,* and author of
The Complete Guide to Horse Careers. She is a contrib-
uting writer to horse magazines such as *Western
Horseman* and *Cascade Horseman*. The story "Jokes 'R
Us" is from the book she co-authored with Tommy

Neiman, *Sirens for the Cross*, which is available from Sue's publishing company, Embrace Communications, 6887 Red Mountain Road, Livermore, Colorado 80536. You can reach Sue at (970) 416-9076 or www.fortnet.org/fcfint/embrace.htm.

Kurt C. Siegel has been a career firefighter and paramedic with the Schenectady Fire Department in Schenectady, New York, since 1980. Currently serving as a captain and EMS coordinator, Kurt also is involved with the New York Regional Response Team-1 (NYRRT-1) Urban Search and Rescue Team as an information specialist. Prior he also served as safety officer and fire department liaison for most of the World Science Fiction Society's North American Conventions in the past decade. Kurt and his wife, Nancy L. Cobb, reside in Schenectady, New York.

Gregg Steward became a firefighter in 1978. Before his promotion to captain with the Costa Mesa Fire Department in Orange County, California, Gregg was a paramedic for thirteen years. He and his wife Bobby have been married for twenty years. They have a sixteen-year-old son.

Robert W. Tennies has been a volunteer firefighter for the last thirteen years with the Hydrant Hose Company No. 1 of the City of Geneva Fire Department in New York. For the last six years he has been a career federal firefighter working at NAS Oceana in Virginia Beach and, currently, Fort Drum, New York. He enjoys spending time with Kaleigh, his six-year-old daughter.

Donna Theisen is an author residing in Fort Myers, Florida. She is a retired EMS professional, author of two books: *Angels of Emergency* and *Childlight*. Donna is currently working on a new book. Presently, Donna is involved in grief counseling for mothers who have lost a child and a member of *Moms On Line*, a support group which helps other grieving mothers deal with their loss. You can e-mail Donna at delaine089@aol.com.

Gary "Tex" Welch was raised in the town of Post, in West Texas. He graduated in 1963 from Texas Tech with a BBA in accounting. During his college years, Tex spent his summers working with the Forest Service, spending most of his time in Cave Junction, Oregon, as a smokejumper. After college, Tex served in the Army as a 2nd lieutenant, where he spent two years in active duty prior to Vietnam. He attended jump school and jumpmaster school during his military training. After he completed his Army service, Tex worked as a National Bank Examiner, eventually running his own bank for twenty years before retiring to run his ranch. He has been enjoying his commercial calf and cow business for the last seven years.

Barry "Skip" Wilson has been a firefighter/paramedic with the Littleton Fire Department in Colorado for the past ten years. He has been involved in EMS since 1976, when he became a Flight-Corpsman with the U.S. Coastguard. He holds a Bachelor of Science Degree in Emergency Medical Services Administration. Skip also is the Juvenile Firesetter Intervention Program coordinator for the Littleton Fire Department. He spends his off-duty time tying flies, fishing, hunting, playing guitar, and raising four rambunctious boys with his wife Sharon. The Wilson family lives in Littleton, Colorado.

Permissions

(continued from page iv)

Nightmare in Oklahoma City. Excerpted from *Angels of Emergency* by Donna Theisen and Dary Matera. ©1996 Donna Theisen & Dary Matera. Published by HarperCollins Publishers. Reprinted by permission.

Is It Worth It? Reprinted by permission of Michael R. Chase. ©2000 Michael R. Chase.

A Life Saved. Reprinted by permission of Doug Faulisi. ©2000 Doug Faulisi.

Weight of the Badge. Reprinted by permission of Michael R. Chase. ©2000 Michael R. Chase.

Emotional Heroes. Reprinted by permission of Barry "Skip" Wilson. ©2000 Barry Wilson.

The Thirteenth Jump. Reprinted by permission of Gary "Tex" Welch. ©2000 Gary Welch.

Flashback. Reprinted by permission of Kurt Seigel. ©2000 Kurt Seigel.

They Emerged from the Smoke. Reprinted by permission of Jim Ellis. ©2000 Jim Ellis.

Once Upon a Time. Reprinted by permission of Michael R. Chase. ©2000 Michael R. Chase.

What Was Her Name? Reprinted by permission of Gary Barr. ©2000 Gary Barr.

Same Old Story. Reprinted by permission. ©1999 Wendy's World.

Gone But Never Forgotten. Reprinted by permisson of Gregg Steward. ©2000 Gregg Steward.

Small World. Reprinted by permission of Michael R. Chase. ©2000 Michael R. Chase.

A Legend in Their Own Time. Reprinted by permission of Johneen Castle. ©2000 Johneen Castle.

Five-Minute Break. Reprinted by permission of Michael R. Chase. ©2000 Michael R. Chase.

Yes, A Cat in the Tree. Reprinted by permission of Tim Miller. ©2000 Tim Miller.

Where Is It? Reprinted by permission of Chuck Fontenot. ©2000 Chuck Fontenot.

The Rookie. Reprinted by permission of Barry "Skip"Wilson. ©2000 Barry "Skip" Wilson.

The Apron. Reprinted by permission of Marc Greenwood. ©2000 Marc Greenwood.

I'm Going to Make it Afterall. Reprinted by permission of Johneen Castle. ©2000 Johneen Castle.

Firefighter, Teacher, Friend. Reprinted by permission of Michael R. Chase. ©2000 Michael R. Chase.

A Silent Alarm. Reprinted by permission of Patricia Rannigan. ©1999 Patricia Rannigan.

No Greater Love. Reprinted by permission of Robert W. Tennies. ©2000 Robert W. Tennies.

You Only Know Him Now. From essay entitled: *A Friend Remembered* by Jon McDuffie. Reprinted by permission of Jon McDuffie. ©1998 Shadoworks™.

Battling the Flames. Reprinted by permission of Timothy C. Cummings. ©1999 Timothy C. Cummings.

Roll of Honor. List of fallen firefighters, from 1981 through 1999, as recognized by the National Fallen Firefighters Foundation. Reprinted by permission of the National Fallen Firefighters Foundation, Emmitsburg, Maryland.

About the
National Fallen Firefighters Foundation

The Heart Behind the Hero publishers have chosen to donate a portion of the proceeds for each book sold to the non-profit organization National Fallen Firefighters Foundation.

The National Fallen Firefighters Memorial was established in 1981. Since that year, names of American fallen firefighters have been added to the monument, located at the *National Fire Academy* in Emmitsburg, Maryland. In 1992, the United States Congress created the National Fallen Firefighters Foundation, expanding the nationwide effort to remember America's fallen firefighters through a variety of activities.

Funding through private donations from individuals and organizations help the Foundation create and support activities that honor America's fallen fire service heroes. These activities include the Annual National Memorial Weekend, scholarships for surviving spouses and children, support programs for survivors, and assistance to fire departments in the handling of line-of-duty deaths.

The Foundation's goal is to memorialize all of America's fallen fire heroes, including those who lost their lives in the line of duty before the creation of the national monument. This would require a team of volunteers throughout the country to research and identify fallen firefighters in each area who died in the line of duty prior to 1981.

Survivors, retired firefighters, ladies auxiliaries, fire departments, and others who wish to volunteer their time to help implement such a program should contact the National Fallen Firefighters Foundation.

For more information about the *National Fallen Firefighters Foundation*, please visit their Website at: www.firehero.org. You also can contact them at:

P.O. Drawer 498, Emmitsburg, Maryland 21727, firehero@erols.com, or call (301) 447-1365.

Additional copies of
The Heart Behind the Hero
may be purchased on-line at
www.firestories.com
or may be ordered by mail using the form
below:

Please send _____ copies of **The Heart Behind the Hero**
at $23.95 each, plus shipping & handling

California residents, please add 7.75% sales tax ($1.86 each).
U.S. shipping: $4.00 for first book ($2.00 each additional).
International shipping: $9.00 for first book ($5.00 each additional).
I understand I may return the book(s) in its original condition
within 30 days for a full refund.

Name: _____

Address: _____

City: _____ State: _____ Zip:

Phone: _____ e-mail address: _____

My payment of $ _____ is being made in the following way:

_____ Check _____ Money Order _____ Visa ___ Master Card

Name of Cardholder: _____

Signature: _____

Card Number: _____ Exp. Date: _____

Mail to:
Stoney Creek Press
P.O. Box 70
Trabuco Canyon, CA 92678-0070
Allow 2 -3 weeks for delivery
Phone & Fax: 1-888-882-1360
E-mail: hero@firestories.com